TELL THEM OF MY GREATNESS

GOD IN THE C-SUITE

DIVINE INFLUENCE DRIVES SUCCESS

Liza Marie Garcia
Bestselling Author

publish@cbpteam.com
www.CEOBookPublishing.com

Ordering Information:

Quantity sales. Special discounts are available on quantity purchases by corporations, associations, and others. For details, contact the publisher at the address above.

Orders by U.S. trade bookstores and wholesalers. Please contact Tel: (813) 970-8470 or visit www.CEOBookPublishing.com

Printed in the United States of America First Printing 2025

ISBN Paperback: 979-8-9927710-6-0
ISBN Hardcover: 979-8-9927710-7-7

Scripture quotations are generally taken from the Holy Bible, New International Version® (NIV) and the English Standard Version (ESV), unless otherwise noted in the text.

All "The Real Story" uses the Message Translations in all chapters

Contents

Introduction

I believe it was 2019. I came home from work in the middle of the day while my daughters were still in school, and I was walking our dog, Snowball Garcia, around the apartment complex. Yes, my two daughters and I were living in a two-bedroom, two-bathroom rented apartment in Carrollwood. This will become significant further along in this book.

As I'm walking Snowball, the yard maintenance folks are loudly cutting the grass and trimming the hedges, and of course, it is one of those absolutely beautiful days in Tampa. I was happily talking with God and feeling grateful for all that was happening in my life. My book publishing business appeared to be well on its way to success, and my two middle school-aged daughters seemed content and happily doing great in school.

As we finished up our walk, I stopped at a very nicely pruned hedge right at the foot of the stairs to our second-story apartment, and I said to God within my spirit, "Wow, God, I can only imagine how awestruck Moses was as you spoke to him from a hedge that was on fire. What thoughts must have run through his head when he noticed no fire anywhere else but the burning bush, as your majestic voice bellowed. What an experience that must have been!"

And then it happened! God answered me so clearly and so plainly that I remember it exactly as if it happened this very morning as I write this. He said directly to me, "Tell them of my greatness!"

I heard His voice, and I knew what He wanted me to do. He wanted me to share what I had been reading about in the Old Testament and what I had been learning from Him in this new chapter of my life in Tampa.

I was inspired and wanted to tell everyone, so they could understand what a mighty, merciful, amazingly loving, father He is.

To help deliver His message. This book presents a series of illustrative case studies and workplace scenarios that highlight the kinds of extraordinary outcomes and breakthrough moments professionals may encounter. While these examples are not drawn from specific individuals, they reflect the types of transformative experiences—often described as miracles—that occur within corporate environments and professional journeys every day. Hopefully, you will be moved by what you read about His greatness all around us in the world today and then you can also spread the good news to others!

Chapter One

The Voice That Shattered Silence

—God Speaks, Then and Now

*"And God said, 'Let there be light,'
and there was light."*

–Genesis 1:3

Long before humanity crafted content or composed award-winning speeches, coached by TedX professionals, there was a voice. Long before there were any professions called "content creators," there was a voice.

A voice so commanding it shattered the void. So powerful it pierced the silence of eternity and set galaxies spinning. This voice was heard by only two people.

That voice was God's.

It wasn't a whisper or a suggestion. It was a decree. "Let there be light." And just like that—light existed. Not because it was summoned from materials. Not because it had somewhere to come from. But because He said so.

It is reported in the Bible that the very first human that heard the voice of God was Adam. Around thirty people in the Old and New Testament are also recorded as speaking with God. They asked and He responded.

Are you someone who can say you have heard His voice? I have. I even shared with those around me how I heard His voice so clearly. A funny thing is that I remember a couple of times I interviewed authors as potential clients for our publishing team, and when they told me they heard the voice of God, I inwardly grimaced in disbelief. Perhaps that is how you feel now, when hearing me share the same message.

His voice, the voice of the God we serve: a God whose words are not commentary, but creation. This voice has unmistakable power.

THE MIRACLE OF SPEECH THAT CREATES

If you're an executive, a professional, a leader, business owner, parent, pastor or even someone working the checkout lane in the supermarket, then you know how much weight words carry.

A single sentence in a Zoom meeting can secure million-plus funding or sink a business partnership. Words can build teams and build people up or divide them. One conversation can spark love, launch conflict, or change lives.

But imagine if your words held the kind of authority God's voice holds.

Genesis doesn't describe God rolling up His sleeves, chiseling out planets, or engineering stars. He simply spoke and reality had to obey. His voice created all the Universe! And do you know that God hasn't ever stopped speaking?

WHEN GOD SPEAKS TO YOU TODAY

God's voice isn't limited to the Garden of Eden or ancient times. He still speaks to all of us all around the globe even today.

He speaks to entrepreneurs on the edge of burnout and to working moms wondering if they've missed their moment. He speaks to all of us at our worst moments and just at the exact time we need Him and long to hear from Him.

He speaks in many ways—through Scripture and that small still voice in your spirit, through dreams, sermons and conversations that stop you in your tracks.

Have you ever had a moment when a verse hit you like it was written just for your situation?

Have you ever had a moment when a verse hit you like it was written just for your situation?

Have you felt the nudge not to take that job, sign that contract, or date that person and only later did you see why?

That's not coincidence. That's the same voice that said, "Let there be light." This is the power of His voice. This is the reason I know beyond any doubt what my purpose in life is.

PROFESSIONAL CASE STUDY: VOICE IN THE CONFERENCE ROOM

Lena, a 41-year-old project manager in Dallas, was in the middle of a high-stakes pitch for a multimillion-dollar partnership. The room was tight. Executives sat stone-faced. Midway through her presentation, she felt a sudden, inexplicable urge to pause.

"Don't push. Pivot."

It wasn't audible. It wasn't logical. But she obeyed. She closed her laptop and began to speak from the heart—about vision, about integrity, about the deeper impact the project would have beyond profit. When she finished, the CEO leaned forward and said, "That's what we needed to hear. We're in."

She told me later, "That wasn't me, that was God. I've never heard Him like that in a meeting before, but I knew it was Him."

CORPORATE CASE STUDY: LEADING WITH LIGHT

When Ava C. took the reins of LumenWorks, the nonprofit with a beautiful mission to bring arts education to underserved schools was stalled, having no sustainable strategy. The books were open, but the future was not. The staff felt adrift. Programs were disjointed. Hope flickered.

Ava didn't start with sweeping changes. She started with light.

Her version of "Let there be light" came in the form of a discovery process she called *The Clarity Initiative*—a series of internal interviews and community engagements to ask: What are we really here to create? Slowly, distinctions emerged. Priorities were established. A shared language began to form.

From light came structure. Ava laid out a phased framework much like the days of creation: separating roles and responsibilities (firmament), building financial foundations (land from water), developing programs that gave measurable impact (sun, moon and stars). With each "day," what was once formless began to take shape.

By year's end, LumenWorks was reporting increased funding, tighter alignment with its stakeholders, and a renewed belief in its creative purpose. Ava liked to say she didn't build something new; she uncovered what was already there, just waiting to be called forth.

The Power That Still Creates

God's voice doesn't just encourage—it creates. It creates peace in your chaos. It creates opportunity in a desert. It creates new beginnings when everyone else sees only endings. It creates the window when the door is shut!

You may not hear thunder or see a burning bush but make no mistake … He's still speaking.

And when He does?

Everything changes.

Reflection

Where in your life do you need to hear God's voice right now?

Are you making space for silence so you can hear Him?

What would change if you trusted that He still speaks with power into your situation?

Prayer

"Lord, speak into my life with the same power that formed the stars. Let Your voice be louder than fear, stronger than doubt, and more real than the noise around me. Help me recognize You when You speak—and give me the courage to do as You will. Amen."

THE REAL STORY: GENESIS 1:1-2:4

1–2 First this: God created the Heavens and Earth—all you see, all you don't see.

Earth was a soup of nothingness, a bottomless emptiness, an inky blackness.

God's Spirit brooded like a bird above the watery abyss.

3–5 God spoke: "Light!"

And light appeared.

God saw that light was good

and separated light from dark.

God named the light Day,

He named the dark Night.

It was evening, it was morning—

Day One.

6–8 God spoke: "Sky! In the middle of the waters;

separate water from water!"

God made sky.

He separated the water under sky

from the water above sky.

And there it was:

He named sky the Heavens;

It was evening, it was morning—

Day Two.

9–10 God spoke: "Separate!

Water-beneath-Heaven, gather into one place;

Land, appear!"

And there it was.

God named the land Earth.

He named the pooled water Ocean.

God saw that it was good.

11–13 God spoke: "Earth, green up! Grow all varieties of seed-bearing plants,

Every sort of fruit-bearing tree."

And there it was.

Earth produced green seed-bearing plants,

All varieties,

And fruit-bearing trees of all sorts.

God saw that it was good.

It was evening, it was morning—

Day Three.

14–15 God spoke: "Lights! Come out!

Shine in Heaven's sky!

Separate Day from Night.

Mark seasons and days and years,

Lights in Heaven's sky to give light to Earth."

And there it was.

16–19 God made two big lights, the larger to take charge of Day,

The smaller to be in charge of Night;

and He made the stars.

God placed them in the heavenly sky to light up Earth

And oversee Day and Night,

To separate light and dark.

God saw that it was good.

It was evening, it was morning—

Day Four.

20–23 God spoke: "Swarm, Ocean, with fish and all sea life!

Birds, fly through the sky over Earth!"

God created the huge whales,

All the swarm of life in the waters,

And every kind and species of flying birds.

God saw that it was good.

God blessed them: "Prosper! Reproduce!

Fill Ocean! Birds, reproduce on Earth!"

It was evening, it was morning—

Day Five.

24–25 God spoke: "Earth, generate life!

Every sort and kind:

Cattle and reptiles and wild animals—all kinds."

And there it was:

Wild animals of every kind,

Cattle of all kinds, every sort of reptile and bug.

God saw that it was good.

26–28 God spoke: "Let us make human beings in our image,

make them reflecting our nature

So they can be responsible for the fish in the sea,

the birds in the air, the cattle,

And, yes, Earth itself,

and every animal that moves on the face of Earth."

God created human beings;

he created them godlike,

Reflecting God's nature.

He created them male and female.

God blessed them:

"Prosper! Reproduce! Fill Earth! Take charge!

Be responsible for fish in the sea and birds in the air,

for every living thing that moves on the face of Earth."

29–30 Then God said, "I've given you

every sort of seed-bearing plant on Earth

And every kind of fruit-bearing tree,

given them to you for food.

To all animals and all birds,

everything that moves and breathes,

I give whatever grows out of the ground for food."

And there it was.

31 God looked over everything He had made;

It was so good, so very good!

It was evening, it was morning—

Day Six.

Heaven and Earth were finished,

down to the last detail.

2-4 By the seventh day

God had finished his work.

On the seventh day

he rested from all his work.

God blessed the seventh day.

He made it a Holy Day

Because on that day he rested from his work,

all the creating God had done.

This is the story of how it all started,

of Heaven and Earth when they were created.

Chapter Two

The Sea That Split for a Slave

—Deliverance Then, Deliverance Now

"Moses answered the people, 'Do not be afraid. Stand firm and you will see the deliverance the Lord will bring you today... The Lord will fight for you; you need only to be still.'"

–Exodus 14:13-14

There's a particular panic that sets in when you're trapped between pressure and a promise.

On one side: the Red Sea—vast, impossible, uncrossable. Really... it's the sea!

On the other: Pharaoh's army—a ton of men, furious, and fast approaching. An entire actual army against you!

The Israelites, as was described in the Old Testament, were just beginning to taste the sweetness of freedom after 400 years of slavery, but now they stood cornered. Nowhere to go, faced with the edge of the water in front of them and the army behind. This scene couldn't have felt more desperate.

What do you do when it seems like your life has led you to a dead end? To yet another disappointment? And how does it feel if you got there because you believed in a dream deep inside you?

It must have been overwhelming, but Moses didn't flinch. He didn't consult a committee; he didn't Facetime anyone for advice or direction. He didn't consult his GPS for another better route, and he definitely didn't start swimming.

Instead, he listened for God, and then he moved at His word.

The sea split. Dry ground appeared. Walls formed across the vast sea and held it back. This all happened by faith, at the command of a benevolent God.

THE GOD WHO STILL PARTS SEAS

Maybe you're not fleeing an Egyptian army, but maybe you feel hemmed in by bills, career burnout, legal battles or deadlines that don't seem to be reachable.

Maybe you finally had the faith to step out of your comfort zone—launched the business, took the risk, hired that new team member and said 'yes' to the call—but now the pressure feels unbearable, like you just can't take it!

Here's what you need to know: God didn't lead you this far to let you drown. God would never give you a dream or goal just to let you fail at it.

You don't need to have the plan.

The same God who made a way through the sea for slaves will make a way for you too.

And here is the big revelation that many people don't know. You don't need to have the plan.

You don't need to figure it out on your own.

You only need to know the God who parts waters.

PROFESSIONAL CASE STUDY: TRAPPED BETWEEN TWO GIANTS

Marianna, a fifty-something-year-old real estate developer in Atlanta, had just invested every dollar she had into a property project that was set to launch with three major investors. Days before closing, one of the backers pulled out. Suddenly, the other two hesitated. Legal threats surfaced. She faced the very real possibility of bankruptcy.

"I was praying, but it felt like shouting into a storm," she said. "I couldn't see any options. I was about to walk away, ashamed and broken."

Then during her morning time with God, she read Exodus 14. The words hit her like lightning, "The Lord will fight for you, you need only to be still."

That day, Marianna stopped calling lawyers. She stopped chasing the issue. She stopped stressing about it and replaying everything that had happened over and over in her head. She prayed and waited. Within 72 hours, a new investor from a completely unrelated industry called out of the blue (someone Marianna had never met), offering to fund the full gap in exchange for minority equity.

"It was as if the sea just opened," she exclaimed, with her eyes tearing up. "And I walked straight through."

CORPORATE CASE STUDY: WALKING INTO THE IMPOSSIBLE

In 2019, a regional hospital network called Harmonia Health Systems found itself squeezed by declining reimbursements and an exodus of frontline staff. Years of underinvestment in digital infrastructure had made coordination clumsy and created an error-prone environment. Meanwhile, new legislation required them to report data they could barely track. Their leaders had two bad options: retreat into risky mergers or face likely collapse.

Enter Dr. Malik, a tenacious yet soft-spoken physician-turned-CEO. On her first day, she told her executive team, "We're not going back to Egypt. The only way out is through."

Dr. Malik initiated what she called *The Red Sea Project*—a radical simplification of their operational model. She began dismantling old hierarchies, empowering cross-functional teams and investing in cloud-based systems that could coordinate real-time care. But resistance was fierce. Critics inside and out scoffed at the fast pace of the changes and the scale of the risk.

Then something unexpected happened: a pilot program they had rolled out on one campus and designed with input from nurses and patients cut ER wait times by 40%. Suddenly, the waters stirred.

The breakthrough didn't come all at once, but like the parted sea, space emerged where there had previously been only chaos. What looked impossible became inevitable, thanks to grit, trust, and leadership that stood still when needed and moved swiftly when the path opened.

Like Moses lifting his staff, Dr. Malik had to signal belief before the evidence appeared. Her story reminds us that sometimes leadership means walking into the impossible—not to avoid fear, but to lead others through it.

The miracle of the Red Sea wasn't just about water moving; it was about God's nature being revealed. He is a Deliverer. A Waymaker, A Promise Keeper. A God who's not intimidated by what intimidates you. In fact, there is nothing in this world that He hasn't planned for and nothing in this world that God isn't in control of. This last fact is something I wish more and more people understood in today's chaotic economy and treacherous global society.

Don't retreat. Don't look back. Don't panic. Stand still. Watch Him work.

My Company's Story: Verizon who?

Years ago, I went through a long and incredibly painful divorce. There were many layers to it, but at the heart of the battle was money. At that point in my life, I wasn't walking with God—I can honestly say I didn't have a real relationship with Him. So, in the midst of the legal fights, the financial fear was overwhelming. I had to buy out my business just to keep it, and when all was said and done, I lost well over seven figures.

But even without a strong connection to God at the time, He was already working behind the scenes. Not even sixty days after I relocated to Tampa, out of nowhere, I was awarded a $500,000-plus contract with Verizon Business. I had never worked with Verizon, never had any ties to them at all. And yet, here it was—this unexpected blessing, worth even more than the final asset settlement from my marriage.

And in that moment, I heard God in my spirit, say.
"Why worry about what you lost? I'm providing you more."

Reflection

What "Red Sea" are you facing right now?

Are you trying to fix things yourself or are you letting God fight for you?

What might God be asking you to do while He prepares the path?

Prayer

"Lord, I feel stuck—cornered by fear, stress, and circumstances beyond my control. But You are the same God who split the sea for Moses. Split my sea too, Lord. Make a way. Teach me to stand still and trust You, even when I can't see the path ahead. Amen."

THE REAL STORY: EXODUS 14:1–31

1–2 GOD spoke to Moses: "Tell the Israelites to turn around and make camp at Pi Hahiroth, between Migdol and the sea. Camp on the shore of the sea opposite Baal Zephon."

3–4 "Pharaoh will think, 'The Israelites are lost; they're confused. The wilderness has closed in on them.' Then I'll make Pharaoh's heart stubborn again and he'll chase after them. And I'll use Pharaoh and his army to put my Glory on display. Then the Egyptians will realize that I am GOD."

And that's what happened.

5–7 When the king of Egypt was told that the people were gone, he and his servants changed their minds. They said, "What have we done, letting Israel, our slave labor, go free?" So he had his chariots harnessed up and got his army together. He took six hundred of his best chariots, with the rest of the Egyptian chariots and their drivers coming along.

8–9 GOD made Pharaoh king of Egypt stubborn, determined to chase the Israelites as they walked out on him without even looking back. The Egyptians gave chase and caught up with them where they had made camp by the sea—all Pharaoh's horse-drawn chariots and their riders, all his foot soldiers there at Pi Hahiroth opposite Baal Zephon.

10–12 As Pharaoh approached, the Israelites looked up and saw them—Egyptians! Coming at them! They were totally afraid. They cried out in terror to GOD. They told Moses, "Weren't the cemeteries large enough in Egypt so that you had to take us out here in the wilderness to die? What have you done to us, taking us out of Egypt? Back in Egypt didn't we tell you this would happen? Didn't we tell you, 'Leave us alone here in Egypt—we're better off as slaves in Egypt than as corpses in the wilderness.'"

13–14 Moses spoke to the people: "Don't be afraid. Stand firm and watch GOD do his work of salvation for you today. Take a good look at the Egyptians today for you're never going to see them again. GOD will fight the battle for you. And you? You keep your mouths shut!"

15–18 GOD said to Moses: "Why cry out to me? Speak to the Israelites. Order them to get moving. Hold your staff high and stretch your hand out over the sea: Split the sea! The Israelites will walk through the sea on dry ground. Meanwhile I'll make sure the Egyptians keep up their stubborn chase—I'll use Pharaoh and his entire army, his chariots and horsemen, to put my Glory on display so that the Egyptians will realize that I am GOD."

19–20 The angel of GOD that had been leading the camp of Israel now shifted and got behind them. And the Pillar of Cloud that had been in front also shifted to the rear. The Cloud was now between the camp of Egypt and the camp of Israel. The Cloud enshrouded one camp in darkness and flooded the other with light. The two camps didn't come near each other all night.

21–22 Then Moses stretched out his hand over the sea and GOD, with a terrific east wind all night long, made the sea go back. He made the sea dry ground. The seawaters split. The Israelites walked through the sea on dry ground with the waters a wall to the right and to the left.

23–25 The Egyptians came after them in full pursuit, every horse and chariot and driver of Pharaoh racing into the middle of the sea. It was now the morning watch. GOD looked down from the Pillar of Fire and Cloud on the Egyptian army and threw them into a panic. He clogged the wheels of their chariots; they were stuck in the mud. The Egyptians said, "Run from Israel! GOD is fighting on their side and against Egypt!"

26–28 GOD said to Moses, "Stretch out your hand over the sea and the waters will come back over the Egyptians, over their chariots, over their horsemen." Moses stretched his hand out over the sea: As the day broke and the Egyptians were running, the sea returned to its place as before. GOD dumped the Egyptians in the middle of the sea. The waters returned, drowning the chariots and riders of Pharaoh's army that had chased after Israel into the sea. Not one of them survived.

29–31 But the Israelites walked right through the middle of the sea on dry ground, the waters forming a wall to the right and to the left. GOD delivered Israel that day from the oppression of the Egyptians. And Israel looked at the Egyptian dead, washed up on the shore of the sea, and realized the tremendous power that GOD brought against the Egyptians. The people were in reverent awe before GOD and trusted in GOD and His servant Moses.

Chapter Three

Manna from Nowhere

—The God of Daily Provision

"Then the Lord said to Moses, 'I will
rain down bread from heaven for you.
The people are to go out each day and
gather enough for that day.'"

–Exodus 16:4

There are seasons when provision feels predictable—paychecks auto deposit on time and cover all your fixed expenses. Financial investments grow, groceries and entertainment budgets are well managed, and for the most part (if we still drive gasoline engine vehicles and not EV's), our tanks are always full.

But what about when all this changes? What about when these provisions vanish?

When the Israelites left Egypt, they had freedom but little or no food. Liberation and a new life had been achieved, but with it came scarcity. It was a completely different landscape for them both literally and figuratively, as they were no longer planting crops or building cities.

What about when all this changes? What about when these provisions vanish?

They were wandering. Hungry. Anxious. Wondering where their next meal would come from.

And then…manna.
Bread. From heaven.
Every morning, just enough. Never too much. Never too little.

That's how God works. Not always early. Never late. But exactly right on time.

Let's go back a moment and make sure, for any of you who haven't read this chapter in the Bible, that you understand a little more about manna. I imagine it as an unleavened type of bread, a large elephant ear-type of flatbread but with little to no seasoning. I wonder what salt or other types of flavors it contained? But this is just my imagined "manna".

This amazing miracle given from God came with a couple of "requirements" I find fascinating. First, it was important that no matter how many people needed to be fed, the exact amount of manna required to feed all persons came down every single day, so no one went hungry. Second, God did not provide manna on the Sabbath, so on the day before, the Israelites would keep a bit of extra manna aside, and it would stay fresh for their Sabbath day portion.

Last, did you know that except for the day before the Sabbath, if the people tried to put aside manna from one day to eat the next day, that manna would go bad and they would not be able to eat it, because it was against God's will?

I love the requirements listed here because it follows a fundamental rule in life, more of everything isn't always better. Trying to take something given as a blessing but manipulate it your own way never leads to success!

WHEN SUCCESS ISN'T ENOUGH

Professionals often live in a high-performance world. You plan, strategize, and build for your career or company growth. You diversify. You protect your intellectual assets, you ensure your accounting is spot on, manage your team, your clients and even your home.

But what happens when success doesn't secure happiness? What if, despite your strategy, there's a spiritual hunger that spreadsheets and software apps can't solve?

In this scenario, God didn't just provide calories in the manna—He taught His people something critical:

"I am your source. Not Egypt. Not men. Not your hustle … Me."

We love God's blessings, but sometimes we cling to the system more than the Source. That's when God leads us into wilderness places—not to punish us, but to remind us of where our provision truly comes from. This might be a more complex concept to grasp today, as it is thousands of years old! However, I can personally understand this struggle.

PERSONAL PROFESSIONAL'S STORY: THE ENVELOPE ON THE DESK

Dana, a 38-year-old attorney from Chicago, had just been laid off from a firm she'd served for over a decade. Two kids, a mortgage, student loans—it all hit her at once. She'd built her life on predictability, and now she was floating in the unknown.

With only a few weeks' worth of savings left, Dana sat at her desk one morning and prayed the desperate prayer so many of us have prayed: "God, I don't have enough. I don't know how I'm going to make it. Please provide."

That same afternoon, she received a call from an old client she hadn't heard from in years. He'd started his own firm and was looking for a partner—someone with her exact background. The retainer he offered was nearly double what she made before.

"I had no résumé ready. I had no plan. I didn't even reach out to him," she told me. "That was manna. Pure manna."

CORPORATE CASE STUDY: STEPPING INTO THE UNKNOWN

When the executive team at GreenWise Analytics launched their transition to a decentralized, agile operations model, many of the staff were anxious. Accustomed to long-term planning cycles and detailed projections, the new environment felt like stepping into the unknown.

Their new COO, Ray P., framed the change in interesting and unexpected terms at the first all-hands meeting: "We're moving from stockpiling certainty to gathering insight daily. We won't have a six-month playbook, but we'll always have what we need for today."

Under his leadership, teams were restructured into smaller, autonomous units with rolling standups. They didn't forecast quarters, they iterated weeks. Their dashboards shifted from lagging indicators to live feedback. In a move that some initially mocked, Ray insisted every department close each Friday with a "Manna Moment" report—a brief reflection on what was learned, what was delivered, and what was enough for that week.

The early results were jarring. Some projects stalled. Others flourished. But over time, something deeper settled in: resilience and confidence. GreenWise didn't just survive the volatile climate of their industry; they began to outperform larger competitors by responding faster to market shifts.

Much like the Israelites learned in the desert, what we need is often granted in measure with our ability to act faithfully on it today. GreenWise learned that their future didn't depend on hoarding resources, but rather on trusting a structure that encouraged responsiveness, community, and just enough light for the next step.

MY COMPANY'S STORY: WAITING ON LATE PAYMENTS

I have a similar personal story to add about waiting on a slow paying client. This payment had been overdue for a month now, and it was my fault for not following up. The amount wasn't huge, but it wasn't super small either. It was money I counted on as part of my family budget to cover basic essentials.

I tried not to focus on the missing money, trust my faith journey, and not let myself get anxious. Then I had a random meeting with a new client. It turned out that she brought a check to sign with us and the amount was within $200 of that invoice amount that was owed to me. My missing budget issue was resolved! This was not a first-time occurrence. I can think of several situations when He provided exactly or even more than I needed at the exact right time.

WHAT MANNA LOOKS LIKE NOW

God's provision today may not fall like pieces of bread from the sky, but it shows up in other, just as miraculous ways:

- A refund you weren't expecting

- A job offer at just the right time

- A medical test that comes back negative

- A neighbor who offers help without being asked

- A person you don't know comes forward to help you, saying "God told me to."

Reflection

Are you relying on God as your Source or have you been trusting data, processes, or people?

What's one area of your life where you need "manna" right now?

Are you looking for tomorrow's answers when God is giving you today's bread?

Prayer

"Father, You are the God who provides. I release my anxiety and fear. You see my needs before I even speak them. Rain down Your provision—whether it's finances, strength, clarity, or favor. Help me trust You for today's manna, knowing You'll show up again tomorrow. Amen."

THE REAL STORY: EXODUS 16:1-36

1-3 On the fifteenth day of the second month after they had left Egypt, the whole company of Israel moved on from Elim to the Wilderness of Sin, which is between Elim and Sinai. The whole company of Israel complained against Moses and Aaron there in the wilderness. The Israelites said,
"Why didn't GOD let us die in comfort in Egypt where we had lamb stew and all the bread we could eat? You've brought us out into this wilderness to starve us to death, the whole company of Israel!"

4 GOD said to Moses, "I'm going to rain bread down from the skies for you. The people will go out and gather each day's ration. I'm going to test them to see if they'll live according to my Teaching or not.

5 On the sixth day, when they prepare what they have gathered, it will turn out to be twice as much as their daily ration."

6-7 Moses and Aaron told the People of Israel, "This evening you will know that it is GOD who brought you out of Egypt; and in the morning you will see the Glory of GOD. Yes, he listens to your complaints against him. You haven't been complaining against us, you know, but against GOD."

8 Moses said, "Since it will be GOD who gives you meat for your meal in the evening and your fill of bread in the morning, it's GOD who will have listened to your complaints against him. Who are we in all this? You haven't been complaining to us—you've been complaining to GOD!"

9-10 Moses instructed Aaron: "Tell the whole company of Israel: 'Come near to GOD. He's heard your complaints.'" When Aaron gave out the instructions to the whole company of Israel, they turned to face the wilderness—and there it was: the Glory of GOD visible in the Cloud.

11-12 GOD spoke to Moses, "I've listened to the complaints of the Israelites. Now tell them, 'At dusk you will eat meat, and at dawn you'll eat your fill of bread. And you'll realize that I am GOD, your God.'"

13-15 That evening quail flew in and covered the camp and in the morning, there was a layer of dew all over the camp. When the layer of dew had lifted, there on the wilderness ground was a fine flaky something, fine as frost on the ground. The Israelites took one look and said to one another, "Man-hu?" (What is it?) They had no idea what it was.
So Moses told them,
"It's the bread GOD has given you to eat."

16 "And these are GOD's instructions: Gather enough for each person, about two quarts per person; gather enough for everyone in your tent."

17-18 The People of Israel went to work and started gathering, some more, some less, but when they measured out what they had gathered, those who gathered more had no extra, and those who gathered less weren't short—each person had gathered as much as was needed.

19 Moses said to them, "Don't leave any of it until morning."

20 But they didn't listen to Moses. A few of them kept back some of it until morning. It got wormy and smelled bad. And Moses lost his temper with them.

21-22 They gathered it every morning, each person according to need. Then the sun heated up and it melted. On the sixth day, they gathered twice as much bread, about four quarts per person.

23 Moses told them,
"This is what GOD was talking about: Tomorrow is a day of rest, a holy Sabbath to GOD. Whatever you plan to bake—bake today; whatever you plan to boil—boil today. Then set aside the leftovers until morning."

24 They set aside what was left until morning, as Moses had commanded. It didn't smell bad and there were no worms in it.

25-26 Moses said, "Now eat it. This is the Sabbath to GOD. You won't find any of it on the ground today. Gather it every day for six days, but the seventh day is the Sabbath; there won't be any of it on the ground."

27-28 On the seventh day, some of the people went out to gather anyway but didn't find anything. GOD said to Moses, "How long are you going to disobey my commands and not follow my instructions?"

29 "Don't you see that GOD has given you the Sabbath? So on the sixth day he gives you bread for two days. So each of you stay home. Don't leave home on the seventh day."

30 So the people quit working on the seventh day.

31 The Israelites called it manna (which means *What is it?*). It looked like coriander seed, whitish, and tasted like a cracker with honey.

32-34 Moses said, "This is GOD's command: Keep a two-quart jar of it as an exhibit for your descendants, so they can see the bread that I fed you in the wilderness when I set you free from Egypt." Moses told Aaron,
"Take a jar and fill it with two quarts of manna. Place it before GOD, keeping it safe for future generations." Aaron did what GOD commanded Moses. He set it aside before The Testimony to preserve it.

35-36 The Israelites ate the manna for forty years until they arrived at the land where they would settle down. They ate manna until they reached the border into Canaan. (According to ancient measurements, an omer is about two quarts.)

Chapter Four

A Wall Came Down with a Shout

—Unseen Power Against Unseen Battles

"When the trumpets sounded, the army shouted, and at the sound of the trumpet, when the men gave a loud shout, the wall collapsed, so everyone charged straight in, and they took the city."

–Joshua 6:20

It was thick. Imposing. Impenetrable.

Jericho's wall didn't just protect a city, it broadcast a message: "You will never pass through here."

And for many of us, that's the message our own "walls" say to us, sometimes over and over.

"You'll never get that position."
"You'll never get married again."

"You'll never get noticed or acknowledged."
"You'll never break that habit."
"You'll never recover."

"You'll never be healed."

But God isn't intimidated by walls.
Not physical ones. Not emotional ones. Not man-made ones, and for sure not the walls made from steel, or even self-doubt.

How this wall came down for Joshua is quite the marvel. God didn't call Joshua to bring it down with an army of construction equipment. God didn't provide the blueprint instructions to break in or map out a siege strategy to take over and occupy. What God told Joshua and His people to do was something that seemed foolish in every professional, military and rational sense. God simply told them to...

March.
Blow horns.
Shout.

And when they obeyed, the wall fell flat. The wall came down right in front of their eyes.

EVIDENCE FIRST

Many of us want God to break down walls **first**, then we'll praise. We want evidence before obedience. We want to make sure what we are doing will result in the outcome we desire, and we want to know things are 100 percent certain before we continue down a difficult road. But faith doesn't work that way.

When God required Joshua and his people to shout before the wall fell down, He was basically asking them to make fools of themselves by trusting God when there was no physical evidence that what they were doing would work. God often calls us to shout in advance, to declare victory before a single brick has moved, before anything in our lives has changed from our perspective.

God often calls us to shout in advance.

In a professional's life, this call to shout might look like:

- Starting a business when the economy is shaky.

- Praising God in the middle of a hiring freeze or when you can't find employment.

- Tithing when the budget says "don't."

- Forgiving someone who hasn't apologized.

- Starting again when a dream you had has died.

Professional Case Study: A Marriage Restored with a Shout

Evan and Monica, a couple in their mid-fifties from Denver, had already spoken to divorce attorneys. Years of resentment had built a thick emotional wall between them. They shared a house but lived like strangers.

Monica, a healthcare executive, started attending a weekly Bible study where someone read the story of Jericho. One phrase stuck with her: *"Shout before the wall falls."*

That night, she did something she hadn't done in months. She sat down beside Evan and looked him in the eyes, and said, "I believe God can tear down this wall if we let Him."

That was her shout.

The healing didn't come instantly, but something began to crack. They started to go to regular counseling and went back to church where prayer returned, and their relationship rekindled.

A year later—standing together next to one another where the wall once stood—they renewed their vows.

"God didn't just knock the wall down," Monica said. "He rebuilt us on new ground."

Corporate Case Study: Bringing Down Barriers

When CEO Dianna T. stepped into her new position, she brought with her something different—not a new tech stack, but a new kind of leadership. She didn't begin with strategy documents. She began with a question: "What walls do you no longer believe can fall?"

She then introduced *The Resonance Program*, a company-wide initiative focused on cultural healing. Daily huddles replaced long memos. Successes were celebrated with actual cheers. Staff were invited to submit "walls" they'd like to see come down—symbolic or structural—and share them out loud at all-hands meetings. The headquarters even installed a "Wall of Jericho" where teams wrote down barriers they were experiencing.

Momentum built slowly, then escalated all at once. Within six months productivity surged, turnover dropped, and teams that hadn't spoken in years began co-creating product lines.

The walls didn't crumble because of a software upgrade. They fell because of *collective voice*, *symbolic rituals*, and *shared vulnerability*. Dianna's insight was simple: unseen battles (resentment, fear, mistrust) require unseen weapons (empathy and unity).

YOUR WALL IS NOT TOO BIG

What wall is standing in your way today?

- A reputation you can't seem to outrun

- A fear you accepted as part of "your journey"

- A judgement from others you accept

- A falseness that you are afraid will be revealed

God is not asking for your perfect plan. He's asking for your faith-filled obedience.

March when He says march.
Shout when He says shout.
And witness what only He can do.

Reflection

What "walls" are you facing in your life, career, or relationships?

Have you been waiting for them to fall before you trust God or are you ready to shout before the miracle happens?

What step of obedience is God asking from you, even if it seems foolish?

Prayer

"Lord, You see the wall I'm facing. It feels too strong, too high, too thick. But I trust You. I will march when You say march, and I will shout when You say shout. I declare that no wall is stronger than Your promise. Tear it down, in Jesus' name. Amen."

THE REAL STORY: JOSHUA 6:1–21

1 Jericho was shut up tight as a drum because of the People of Israel: no one going in, no one coming out.

2 GOD spoke to Joshua, "Look sharp now. I've already given Jericho to you, along with its king and its crack troops.

3-5 Here's what you are to do: March around the city, all your soldiers. Circle the city once. Repeat this for six days. Have seven priests carry seven ram's horn trumpets in front of the Chest. On the seventh day, march around the city seven times, the priests blowing away on the trumpets. And then a long blast on the ram's horn—when you hear that, all the people are to shout at the top of their lungs. The city wall will collapse at once. All the people are to enter, every man straight on in."

6-7 So Joshua, the son of Nun, called the priests and told them, "Take up the Chest of the Covenant. Seven priests are to carry seven ram's horn trumpets leading GOD's Chest." Then he told the people, "Set out! March around the city. Have the armed guard march before the Chest of GOD."

8-9 And it happened. Joshua spoke, the people moved: Seven priests with their seven ram's horn trumpets set out before GOD. They blew the trumpets, leading GOD's Chest of the Covenant. The armed guard marched ahead of the trumpet-blowing priests, the rear guard was marching after the Chest, marching and blowing, marching and blowing.

10 Joshua had given orders to the people, "Don't shout. In fact, don't even speak—not so much as a whisper until you hear me say, 'Shout!'—then shout away!"

11 He sent the Chest of GOD on its way around the city. It circled once, came back to camp, and stayed for the night.

12-13 Joshua was up early the next morning, and the priests took up the Chest of GOD. The seven priests carrying the seven ram's horn trumpets marched before the Chest of GOD, marching and blowing the trumpets, the armed guard marching before them and the rear guard marching after the Chest, marching and blowing, marching and blowing.

14 On the second day they again circled the city once and returned to camp. They did this for six days.

15 When the seventh day came, they got up early and marched around the city this way seven times. Yes, this day they circled the city seven times.

16 On the seventh time around, the priests blew the trumpets and Joshua signaled the people, "Shout!—GOD has given you the city!

17-19 The city and everything in it is under a holy curse and offered up to GOD. Except for Rahab the harlot—she is to live, she and everyone in her house with her, because she hid the agents we sent. As for you, watch yourselves in the city under holy curse—be careful that you don't covet and take anything that's under the holy curse and make the camp of Israel itself cursed and troubled. All silver and gold, all vessels of bronze and iron are holy to GOD. Put them in GOD's treasury."

20 The priests blew the trumpets. As soon as the people heard the blast of the trumpets, they gave a loud shout, and the wall collapsed! They ran straight into the city and captured it.

21 They put everything in the city under the holy curse, killing man and woman, young and old, ox and sheep and donkey.

Chapter Five

Water into Wine
in the Boardroom

—The God Who Elevates the Ordinary

"Jesus said to the servants, 'Fill the jars with water'; so they filled them to the brim. Then He told them, 'Now draw some out and take it to the master of the banquet.'"

–John 2:7-8

It was supposed to be a celebration, but behind the laughter, something embarrassing was happening.

The wine ran out.

And in that culture, to run out of wine at a wedding wasn't just a social inconvenience, it was a public disgrace. It meant poor planning, lack of resources and shame for the host. It could be likened to running out of food at a gala fundraising event or the bartenders not showing up at an event where tickets for alcohol were purchased in advance.

But more than this embarrassment, during those times it was a complete dishonor and shameful circumstance if the host ran out of wine, especially at a wedding.

Have you ever had something "run out" in front of people who were counting on you? Perhaps you had ideas dry up in the middle of a conference? Maybe you ran out of energy before the workday was over. (This one happens to me quite often, it seems, and I never seem to have any caffeine handy.)

He didn't criticize. He didn't panic. He didn't even make a scene.

Have all your company's resources been exhausted just before the project or deal was done? It could even be something as common as losing confidence while in the middle of a speaking event.

That's what happened at this wedding in Cana.

But then Jesus did something unexpected. He didn't criticize. He didn't panic. He didn't even make a scene. He quietly asked for water.

The most basic, everyday, unimpressive item. Tap water, no less. It was nothing in a fancy box, not sparkling, not designer water, just the most basic resource we have … water. But then, He turned it into wine.

And not just any wine—the best wine. Because that's who He is. The God who transforms ordinary into excellence.

EXCELLENCE THROUGH OBEDIENCE

Notice something powerful, before the miracle happened, Jesus gave a strange instruction.

"Fill the jars with water." Not "pray harder." Not "find more grapes." Just obey with what you have. Sometimes your miracle is simply waiting for your action.

What if your next breakthrough doesn't come from working harder. Could it come from listening closer?

PROFESSIONAL CASE STUDY: A STARTUP'S SUPERNATURAL SHIFT

David, a 31-year-old tech entrepreneur from Seattle, had poured every resource he had into developing a mental wellness app. But after a year of working nonstop, he wasn't gaining traction. His investors were growing silent. Downloads were flatlining. The "wine" had run out.

One night, after a particularly disappointing call, David sat in his office and asked God, "What now?" And in the stillness, he felt this phrase press into his heart:

"Use what's in your hand."

It didn't make sense at first, but then he remembered a content idea he'd shelved months earlier … simple 60-second encouragements for high-performing professionals. It felt too basic, too watered-down. But he obeyed and uploaded one short video, then another.

Within 30 days, the app's traffic surged by over 400%. Users began citing his clips as daily lifelines. One Fortune 100 company reached out to offer a partnership for employee wellness. The wine came rushing back.

"All I did was offer God the water," David said. "And He turned it into something I couldn't have created on my own."

CORPORATE CASE STUDY: ACTING WITH DELIBERATE ATTENTIVENESS

At BlueNova Hospitality Group, a boutique hotel chain known for elegant simplicity, a different kind of celebration was running dry. After years of pandemic challenges and staff attrition, guest satisfaction had flattened, and employee morale had taken a quiet tumble. Everything looked fine on paper—occupancy was steady, reviews decent—but something vital was missing.

CEO Lillian N. saw the warning signs, but instead of sweeping changes or splashy marketing, she began with a simple directive: *"Fill the jars."*

Her version? A return to daily excellence. Lillian asked every property GM to gather their teams and identify one overlooked area where they could restore a sense of care—whether with a turndown service, handwritten notes, or the scent of the lobby at check-in. She encouraged departments to act with deliberate attentiveness, even when they didn't see immediate results.

A curious thing happened. Small rituals, like housekeepers restocking coffee "to the brim," or concierges offering local handwritten guides, began to shift the atmosphere. Then a single gesture—an assistant night manager arranging a sunrise rooftop breakfast for a grieving widow—went viral on social media.

The hotel didn't change overnight. But its *water quietly became wine.* It was a transformation born not of spectacle, but of daily obedience and hidden care. Lillian often reflected: "The miracle wasn't in the wine. It was in the willingness to pour faithfully, before knowing what it would become."

SCALING THE SACRED – EMBEDDING RITUAL INTO REPUTATION

After the initial ripple of transformation, Lillian recognized something essential: the miracle wasn't a one-time story, but a repeatable rhythm. She convened a leadership retreat, titled *"From Jars to Joy,"* to ask a defining question: *How do we scale the soul without losing the sincerity?*

The answer wasn't found in policies; it was found in *patterns*.

Lillian and her team codified a framework called *BRIM*, inspired by Jesus' command to "fill the jars to the brim." It wasn't a checklist; it was a compass. *BRIM* encouraged four pillars:

1. **Behold the Guest** — see beyond the transaction to the story.

2. **Respond with Wonder** — treat each moment as sacred, not routine.

3. **Imprint the Senses** — use beauty, fragrance, warmth to craft experiences.

4. **Manifest the Invisible** — honor the unseen labor that makes delight possible.

Rather than force compliance, *BRIM* empowered teams to *reinterpret the framework within their own property's soul.* A mountaintop retreat cabin introduced personalized firewood bundles with guests' initials, while a city hotel curated pocket-sized art maps with entries drawn by local schoolchildren.

Even internal communications shifted. Quarterly updates opened with "Modern Miracles"—real staff-submitted stories of ordinary service that had unexpected meaning.

Within a year, BlueNova's Net Promoter Score rose by 18 points, employee retention improved dramatically and their "BRIM Moments" series became a staple in hospitality leadership talks.

The brilliance of the Cana story wasn't just in the wine—it was that transformation happened without spectacle, *through vessels already in the room, filled by ordinary people, used in extraordinary ways.*

THE MIRACLE ISN'T ALWAYS LOUD

Not every miracle is fire-from-heaven or sea-splitting drama. Some of the most powerful ones happen quietly, in the margins so to speak, in zoom meetings, in our (junk folders) emails. Sometimes the whisper of an idea turns everything around.

Jesus didn't need a spotlight to transform the wedding. What He needed was just someone willing to fill the jars. What jars do you have?

What skill, connection, resource or routine have you overlooked because it feels too ordinary? You have determined the problem couldn't be solved so easily so you dismissed it. Don't do this over and over again … put it in His hands.

Reflection

What feels "empty" in your life or career right now?

Are you willing to bring your ordinary, your water, to Jesus and let Him make it extraordinary?

Where might God be asking you to obey something simple and that doesn't make much sense to you today?

Prayer

"Lord, I've been trying to make something out of nothing. I'm tired. But I bring You what I have, even if it feels small or unimpressive. Transform it, God. Turn water into wine in my life, in my work, in my heart. I trust You with the ordinary. Amen."

The Real Story: John 2:1-11

1-3 Three days later there was a wedding in the village of Cana in Galilee. Jesus' mother was there. Jesus and his disciples were guests also. When they started running low on wine at the wedding banquet, Jesus' mother told him, "They're just about out of wine."

4 Jesus said, "Is that any of our business, Mother—yours or mine? This isn't my time. Don't push me."

5 She went ahead anyway, telling the servants, "Whatever he tells you, do it."

6-7 Six stoneware water pots were there, used by the Jews for ritual washings. Each held twenty to thirty gallons.
Jesus ordered the servants, "Fill the pots with water."
And they filled them to the brim.

8 "Now fill your pitchers and take them to the host," Jesus said, and they did.

9-10 When the host tasted the water that had become wine, he didn't know what had just happened (but the servants, of course, knew). He called out to the bridegroom, "Everybody I know begins with their finest wines and after the guests have had their fill brings in the cheap stuff. But you've saved the best till now!"

11 This act in Cana of Galilee was the first sign Jesus gave, the first glimpse of his glory. And His disciples believed in Him.

Chapter Six

Bones That Lived Again

—Resurrecting What You Thought Was Over

"Then He said to me, 'Prophesy to these bones and say to them, "Dry bones, hear the word of the Lord! I will make breath enter you, and you will come to life."

–Ezekiel 37:4-5

Imagine walking through a valley full of bones.

No flesh. No life. No sound. Just the silence of something that used to be.

This is the scene God brought Ezekiel into—a place of former strength, now reduced to dry remains. These weren't just bones; they were hopes that had died. Potential that had decayed. A people who had once thrived, now silent, buried and broken.

And then God asked a wild question:

"Can these bones live?"

Ezekiel didn't say "yes" or "no." He gave the only answer that makes sense when you're standing in front of a dead thing:

Potential that had decayed.

"Sovereign Lord, only You know."

Because only God can look at what we've buried and see a blueprint for resurrection.

YOUR VALLEY MIGHT STILL BREATHE

Every professional, at some point, walks through a "valley of dry bones."

- The business you started that went under

- The promotion you didn't get—again

- The ministry that fizzled

- The friendship that died

- The version of yourself you don't recognize anymore

And we say things like,

"It's over."

"I missed my window."

"I should've known better."

"That part of me is gone."

But God is not finished with what looks finished to you. He doesn't need fresh clay. He can rebuild from dry bones.

All He needs is your faith to speak.

PROPHECY COMES BEFORE PROGRESS

Notice what God told Ezekiel to do:

"Prophesy to these bones…"

Speak life before you see life.
Declare truth before anything moves.
Call out purpose in a place that looks pointless.

Why? Because when we partner with God's word, heaven invades what hell tried to erase.

This is where revival begins—in your voice, in your worship, in your willingness to believe that dead isn't done.

PROFESSIONAL CASE STUDY: A MUSIC CAREER REBORN AT 60

Vivian, a 60-year-old retired music teacher from Charlotte, NC, had stopped writing songs decades ago. She'd raised kids, cared for aging parents and built a life of service. But the part of her that created—the part that dreamed—felt buried.

One Sunday morning during worship, she felt God whisper, *"I never told you to stop singing."* That week, she dusted off her old keyboard and wrote her first song in over 20 years.

She uploaded a simple video to YouTube.

Within a month, her song was picked up by a Christian indie label looking for "raw, real, anointed voices."

Today, she's released two albums and leads worship for a multi-generational online community. "I thought I was too old. Too late," Vivian says. "Turns out God just needed me to speak to the bones."

CORPORATE CASE STUDY: REIMAGINED AND REBUILT

Ezekiel saw bones—dry, brittle, forgotten—but in them, God saw an army. The transformation didn't begin with infrastructure; it began with *words*. With vision. With someone bold enough to speak life into what others called dead.

Such was the story behind ReviveMotion, once a promising fitness tech startup that had nearly faded from the landscape. After two failed product launches, critical staff departures and a highly publicized lawsuit over intellectual property, the company's future was declared "beyond resuscitation" by industry analysts. Investors walked. Staff scattered. Their offices sat mostly dark.

But co-founder Aisha M. couldn't shake the sense that the company wasn't truly dead—just disconnected from its breath.

She returned not with capital, but with conviction. In a quiet corner of their abandoned HQ, Aisha invited the last remaining seven employees to a whiteboard/workshop session. She scribbled one word, *Prophesy*. "Speak what you once believed," she urged. "What did we exist to do before we collapsed under fear?"

One by one, the team revisited the original mission: holistic wellness tech that empowered rather than pressured. The idea wasn't dead. It had been buried beneath over-engineering and market noise.

They didn't relaunch immediately. They listened. Reimagined. Rebuilt. They reached out to former users, asking what they *missed*. Then came the breath when a new, stripped-down prototype unexpectedly trended among fitness influencers for its simplicity and mental health integrations.

Three months later, ReviveMotion reemerged—not with a splashy campaign, but with an authentic, quiet rebirth. The bones had heard the word and breath had entered.

The lesson? When hope looks like rubble, speak purpose. Prophesy to the bones. Even dry ones remember who they were made to be.

WHAT ARE YOU AFRAID TO RESURRECT?

What have you given up on because it didn't happen on *your* timeline?

- That book you started writing
- That dream to lead
- That burden to mentor or teach
- That relationship you stopped praying for
- That business idea that once made your heart leap

Maybe it's time to stop burying what God still wants to breathe into.

Your valley isn't the end. It might just be the birthplace of a miracle.

Reflection

What part of your life feels like a "valley of dry bones" right now?

Have you stopped speaking life over something God never told you to abandon?

What would it look like to *prophesy to the bones* this week?

Prayer

"God, I give You every place in my life that feels dry, forgotten, or too far gone. I speak life over what I thought was dead. Resurrect what I buried. Revive my dreams. Restore my hope. You are the God who makes bones live again, and I believe You can do it in me. Amen."

The Real Story: Ezekiel 37:1–14

1–2 God grabbed me. God's Spirit took me up and set me down in the middle of an open plain strewn with bones. He led me around and among them—a lot of bones! There were bones all over the plain—dry bones, bleached by the sun.

3 He said to me, "Son of man, can these bones live?"
I said, "Master God, only You know that."

4–6 He said to me, "Prophesy over these bones: 'Dry bones, listen to the Message of God!'"

God, the Master, told the dry bones: **"Watch this: I'm bringing the breath of life to you and you'll come to life.**
I'll attach sinews to you, put meat on your bones, cover you with skin, and breathe life into you.
You'll come alive and you'll realize that I am God!"

7–8 I prophesied just as I'd been commanded.
As I prophesied, there was a sound and, oh!—a rustling! The bones moved and came together, bone to bone.
I kept watching. Sinews formed, then muscles on the bones, then skin stretched over them.
But they had no breath in them.

9–10 He said to me, "Prophesy to the breath. Prophesy, son of man. Tell the breath, 'God, the Master, says, Come from the four winds. Come, breathe. Breathe on these slain bodies. Breathe life!'"
So I prophesied, just as He commanded me.
The breath entered them and they came alive!
They stood up on their feet, a huge army.

11–14 Then God said to me, "Son of man, these bones are the whole house of Israel. Listen to what they're saying: 'Our bones are dried up, our hope is gone, there's nothing left of us.' Therefore, prophesy. Tell them, 'God, the Master, says: I'll dig up your graves and bring you out alive—O my people!

Then I'll take you straight to the land of Israel.

When I dig up graves and bring you out as my people, you'll realize that I am God.

I'll breathe my life into you and you'll live. Then I'll lead you straight back to your land and you'll realize that I am God. I've said it and I'll do it. God's Decree.'"

Chapter Seven

Fire That Didn't Burn

—Faith That Walks Through Flames

"And the satraps, prefects, governors and royal advisers crowded around them. They saw that the fire had not harmed their bodies, nor was a hair of their heads singed; their robes were not scorched, and there was no smell of fire on them."

–Daniel 3:27

At work, do you feel like sometimes the pressure is so real, it feels like you're living in a furnace? Do you feel like there is nothing that can save you, because you are in so deep the pressure is so real it's super-hot!

Could it be any one of these?

- Deadlines that won't stop coming at you

- Tension with a business partner, teammate, or your direct report manager

- Financial pressure that keeps tightening and it seems like nothing can help you catch up

- Mental burnout that no one sees, no one can understand

Shadrach, Meshach and Abednego knew what that felt like—literally. Thrown into a blazing furnace for refusing to bow to a lie, they walked into fire because they chose truth over comfort. But what happened next changed history.

They didn't burn, they didn't break, they didn't even smell like smoke, because someone else was in the fire with them.

"Look! I see four men walking around in the fire… and the fourth looks like a son of the gods!" —Daniel 3:25

That fourth man? Jesus showing up in the middle of the heat.

They didn't burn, they didn't break, they didn't even smell like smoke

God Doesn't Always Deliver You *From* the Fire… But Always He is in it with you.

The problem most of the time, is that we want rescue before the flames. We try to figure things out all on our own, based on the past and how we believe we could struggle through. But in this story, these three men didn't have a Plan B. They weren't negotiating with God. They said, *"Even if He does not [rescue us], we will not bow."*

Not only were they in the fire, but their faith was also on fire.

It's easy to believe we can help ourselves out of any pressure cooker at some point, but what if we decide to change this thinking and understand that He is the only one who can get us out of the fire. He is the one that will be with us to walk us right out of any pressure situation.

PROFESSIONAL CASE STUDY: PROTECTED IN THE CORPORATE FIRESTORM

Manny, a 47-year-old VP at a national marketing firm in San Jose, CA, was asked to sign off on a project pitch that manipulated key performance data. It was subtle, but in the end, it was dishonest.

"I knew approving this pitch would make me look like a team player," he said, "but I also knew it was a lie." He decided to decline and not put his name behind it.

A few weeks later, a formal ethics review at his company exposed the deception and vindicated his integrity. His boldness sparked a quiet culture shift within his division, and within six months, he was offered a promotion with greater influence.

He could've bowed but he chose the fire. And in the end, God stood with him in it.

CORPORATE CASE STUDY: WALKING THROUGH THE FIRE

Eric was the Chief Operations Officer of a mid-sized logistics company based in Wyoming. He had spent 18 years building his reputation—someone who delivered results, kept promises, and led with character. But when his CEO asked him to "massage" supplier audit results to avoid losing a major client, he felt the furnace roar to life.

"It wasn't illegal," he recalls, "but it was dishonest. I knew once I said 'no,' everything could change." And it did. Eric was quietly sidelined from executive meetings, his responsibilities were reassigned, and team members were told he was "taking a step back for personal reasons." He wasn't fired—but it felt worse. Invisible. Powerless. Alone.

But he wasn't alone.

Two months later, that same client conducted an independent audit—and found the very issues Eric had refused to cover up. His integrity became the company's lifeline. Within weeks, the board requested a leadership transition, and Eric was appointed interim CEO. His reward wasn't just a new title; it was the testimony of walking through the fire and not even smelling like smoke.

You Don't Need to Escape—You Need to Endure

Maybe you've been praying for God to *remove* the fire, but maybe this is really the wrong prayer. Shouldn't your prayer be to preserve you inside the fire?

Maybe your greatest testimony is formed in the heat. Sometimes, pressure is the proving ground for promotion. And when you come out of the fire, just like those three Hebrew men, you won't even smell like smoke.

Reflection

What fire are you currently walking through at work?

Are you tempted to bow to something that goes against your beliefs or values?

Can you recognize God is *with you* in the middle of the fires?

Prayer

"Jesus, thank You that I never walk through fire alone. When the heat is on, when the pressure rises, when the threats come—I know You are in it with me. Strengthen my resolve. Protect my mind, my peace, my purpose. And when I come out, let there be no smoke on me! Amen."

THE REAL STORY: DANIEL 3

1 King Nebuchadnezzar built a gold statue, ninety feet high and nine feet thick. He set it up on the Dura plain in the province of Babylon.

2 He then ordered all the important leaders in the province, everybody who was anybody, to the dedication ceremony of the statue.

3 They all came for the dedication, all the important people, and took their places before the statue that Nebuchadnezzar had erected.

4 A herald then proclaimed in a loud voice: "Attention, everyone! Every race, color, and creed, listen!

5 When you hear the band strike up—all the trumpets and trombones, the tubas and baritones, the drums and cymbals— fall to your knees and worship the gold statue that King Nebuchadnezzar has set up.

6 Anyone who does not kneel and worship shall be thrown immediately into a roaring furnace."

7 The band started to play, a huge band equipped with all the musical instruments of Babylon, and everyone—every race, color, and creed—fell to their knees and worshiped the gold statue that King Nebuchadnezzar had set up.

8 Just then, some Babylonian fortunetellers stepped up and accused the Jews.

9 They said to King Nebuchadnezzar, "Long live the king!

10 You gave strict orders, O king, that when the big band started playing, everyone had to fall to their knees and worship the gold statue,

11 and whoever did not go to their knees and worship it had to be pitched into a roaring furnace.

12 Well, there are some Jews here—Shadrach, Meshach, and Abednego—whom you have placed in high positions in the province of Babylon. These men are ignoring you, O king. They don't respect your gods and they won't worship the gold statue you set up."

13 Furious, King Nebuchadnezzar ordered Shadrach, Meshach, and Abednego to be brought in. When the men were brought in,

14 Nebuchadnezzar asked, "Is it true, Shadrach, Meshach, and Abednego, that you don't respect my gods and refuse to worship the gold statue that I have set up?

15 I'm giving you a second chance—but from now on, when the big band strikes up you must go to your knees and worship the statue I have made. If you don't worship it, you will be pitched into a roaring furnace, no questions asked. Who is the god who can rescue you from my power?"

16 Shadrach, Meshach, and Abednego answered King Nebuchadnezzar, "Your threat means nothing to us.

17 If you throw us in the fire, the God we serve can rescue us from your roaring furnace and anything else you might cook up, O king.

18 But even if He doesn't, it wouldn't make a bit of difference, O king. We still wouldn't serve your gods or worship the gold statue you set up."

19 Nebuchadnezzar, his face purple with anger, cut off Shadrach, Meshach, and Abednego. He ordered the furnace fired up seven times hotter than usual.

20 He ordered some strong men from the army to tie them up, hands and feet, and throw them into the roaring furnace.

21 Shadrach, Meshach, and Abednego, bound hand and foot, fully dressed from head to toe, were pitched into the roaring fire.

22 Because the king was in such a hurry and the furnace was so hot, flames from the furnace killed the men who carried Shadrach, Meshach, and Abednego to it,

23 while the fire raged around Shadrach, Meshach, and Abednego.

24 Suddenly King Nebuchadnezzar jumped up in alarm and said, "Didn't we throw three men, bound hand and foot, into the fire?" "That's right, O king," they said.

25 "But look!" he said. "I see four men, walking around freely in the fire, completely unharmed! And the fourth man looks like a son of the gods!"

26 Nebuchadnezzar went to the door of the roaring furnace and called in, "Shadrach, Meshach, and Abednego, servants of the High God, come out here!" Shadrach, Meshach, and Abednego walked out of the fire.

27 All the important people, the government leaders and king's counselors, gathered around to examine them and discovered that the fire hadn't so much as touched the three men—not a hair singed, not a scorch mark on their clothes, not even the smell of fire on them!

28 Nebuchadnezzar said, "Blessed be the God of Shadrach, Meshach, and Abednego! He sent His angel and rescued His servants who trusted in Him! They ignored the king's orders and laid their bodies on the line rather than serve or worship any god but their own."

Chapter Eight

Faith Pulls Power

—Desperation, What It Leads To

"She said to herself, 'If I only touch His cloak, I will be healed.'"

–Matthew 9:21

Twelve years. That's how long she suffered.

For twelve years she suffered from uncontrollable bleeding, which was highly embarrassing and created for her the need to isolate. She sought out doctor after doctor for help, and spent all her money, but with no cure.

This twelve years of being labeled "unclean" affected her not just physically, but socially and mentally, as well.

She had every reason to give up. To stop believing things would ever change, but she didn't.

She thought, *"If I can just touch the hem of His garment…"*

Not His hand, not His face, just the edge of what He was wearing—hoping that any part of something so amazing could be the answer to her prayers. She was right. The moment she touched Him, everything changed. That was the moment she was healed.

WHEN YOU'VE TRIED EVERYTHING ELSE

The theme of this woman's story happens every day to regular people, who have tried every self-help strategy they could find. What about when you've tried to gain new clients by networking, and pitching, but new doors stay shut? You've even prayed, but it seems heaven's been silent.

That's where she was—exhausted but still reaching.

You're tired, but hopefully not faithless. That's where she was—exhausted but still reaching. And that reach moved Jesus. *"Who touched Me?"* He asked.

Jesus's disciples were confused because *everyone* was touching Him. But her faith in the end, pulled healing power she needed.

Because **faith pulls power.**

PERSONAL PROFESSIONAL'S STORY: HEALING IN A WAITING ROOM

Sandra, a 39-year-old corporate attorney from Chicago, battled chronic autoimmune issues for years. She had the best doctors, access to cutting-edge treatments, and still no relief. Quietly, she began to sink into anxiety and depression, although few around her knew it.

One day, while waiting for yet another specialist, she opened her Bible app and read the story about the woman with the bleeding issue.

Sandra whispered: *"God, I'm tired. But I still believe. Just let me touch You today."*

As she sat in that sterile office, she felt what she described as "a calm wash over me, like I was being filled from the inside out." She didn't hear angels. The diagnosis didn't vanish. But from that moment forward, her symptoms began to steadily reverse.

Today, she's been symptom-free for over four years. "It wasn't instantaneous," she said, "but it was real."

CORPORATE CASE STUDY: REACHING FOR SOMETHING BIGGER

In early 2020, a well-respected mid-size consulting firm based in San Antonio found itself in a downward spiral. After two consecutive years of declining revenue, multiple failed rebranding attempts, and a mass client exodus, morale was at an all-time low. Employees were anxious. Leadership was stretched thin. And behind closed doors, the executive team began quietly discussing a possible shutdown or sell-off.

Karrin, the newly appointed CEO, had been brought in as a last-hope leader. She was known for her turnaround expertise, but even she admitted, "We had tried everything. Every strategic lever had been pulled—cost-cutting, restructuring, new market positioning—but nothing was working."

What no one on the outside saw was the spiritual desperation growing behind the scenes.

"I remember walking into the boardroom one morning and thinking, *If something doesn't break soon, this company won't make it through the quarter,*" Karrin shared. That night, after working late in her office, she sat alone and opened her Bible to Matthew 9. She wasn't looking for business advice—she was just searching for hope.

"If I only touch His cloak, I will be healed."

That verse hit her like lightning. "I realized—I'd been relying on my own strength, experience, and tools. I hadn't once asked God to touch this business."

The next day, she gathered her senior leadership team and did something unheard of in their corporate culture: she invited them to pray. Not a religious ritual, but an honest cry for help. "We didn't ask God to fix our problems—we simply said, *We need You in this boardroom. We can't do this without You.*"

That moment marked a turning point. Not immediately, but undeniably.

Over the next 12 months:

- An unexpected referral brought in their largest client in five years.

- A former competitor proposed a strategic alliance that opened new revenue streams.

- Their company culture transformed—from fear-driven to faith-infused.

Today, that same firm has doubled in size and now operates in three new markets. "Our healing didn't come through a single hire or idea," Karrin says. "It came when we finally reached for something bigger than ourselves."

Reflection

What area of your life feels like a twelve-year issue—long, painful, private?

Have you stopped reaching because nothing seems to change?

Are you willing to stretch your faith one more time?

Prayer

"Jesus, I don't have strength to shout or strive. But I still believe. I believe I can reach for You, not just for show, but for survival. Just one touch from You can change everything. I trust that You see me, You love me, and only You can respond to even the faintest touch of faith. Amen."

THE REAL STORY: MATTHEW 9

The Issue of Blood

19 Jesus got up and went with him, his disciples following along.

20 Just then a woman who had hemorrhaged for twelve years slipped in from behind and lightly touched his robe.

21 She was thinking to herself, "If I can just put a finger on his robe, I'll get well." Jesus turned—caught her at it. Then he reassured her: "Courage, daughter. You took a risk of faith, and now you're well."

22 The woman was well from then on.

Chapter Nine

Fed in the Wilderness

—Who Provides Where Nothing Can Grow?

*"Then the LORD said to Moses,
'I will rain down bread from heaven for you.'"*
–Exodus 16:4

There's a kind of obedience that's exciting. Then there's the kind that's… *terrifying*. The Israelites followed God out of Egypt after experiencing firsthand all sorts of miracles that were still fresh in their minds. The plagues, a parting of the seas … it must have been thrilling and definitely a victory for the Israelites.

But as a little time went by and they walked into their new "chapter," reality set in. They were in a desert now. There were no farms, no fountains and definitely no food.

From their perspective, they obeyed God, and for this they ended up in the wilderness.

Have you ever complied with everything required of you, but then landed in a place that made you question everything? Have you obeyed God but were left with a bewildered frame of mind?

Did you leave a job because you knew God told you to, but now you're staring at bills that are real. Or perhaps you launched the business in faith, but the numbers aren't adding up.

I myself felt compelled to move across the United States, but then I felt lost and unsupported.

The wilderness is real. But it's often preparation, not a punishment.

MIRACLES IN STRANGE PLACES

God didn't say, "Oops, my bad. Let Me lead you back to Egypt." Instead, He said, *"I'll feed you right here."* Not in a kitchen, not through predictable food sources. There were no Uber Eats.

They were in a wilderness—no harvests, no stores or no irrigation. And yet, heaven opened and manna fell—not because the people had planned well, but because God provides where nothing else can.

Professional Case Study: God Sent Clients

Jason, a 52-year-old freelance graphic designer from Houston, had worked with a high-paying agency for nearly a decade. When he felt God leading him to step away and go solo, he hesitated but eventually obeyed. For months, he barely made enough to survive. He prayed. Fasted. He even updated his resume, but nothing worked.

Then one Sunday, during a quiet time with God, he heard a whisper: *"You're in the wilderness, but I'm not done feeding you."* That week, he received three unsolicited referrals, none from his network. His client load tripled within a month. "I thought I'd have to grind my way to survival," Jason said. "But God reminded me that He doesn't need my grind. He needs my trust."

CORPORATE CASE STUDY: FAILURE BECAME A FOUNDATION

In 2021, Terra AgroTech found itself in a commercial drought of its own. Its flagship soil revitalization product, designed to support drought-ridden farmlands, had failed to gain traction in its original North American markets. Regulatory delays, depleted reserves, and growing skepticism among their investors painted a bleak picture. Then the most unlikely call came from Mongolia.

An environmental coalition from the Gobi Desert reached out, intrigued by Terra's claims that their biotechnologies could improve soil viability in semi-arid zones. The team at headquarters was stunned. Their testing had never focused on regions with so little precipitation or organic matter. "Nothing grows there," one board member muttered.

But CEO Jonah R. heard something else: *manna in the wilderness.*

With little capital, Terra sent a tiny pilot team—three scientists, one agronomist and a local translator. They partnered with nomadic communities, tested treatments on desolate patches of land, and waited. Growth was slow, but then it came. Tufts of barley and hardy legumes emerged where dust had once ruled. Local herders wept. The project, documented by an independent NGO, went viral.

Within a year, Terra had secured multi-nation funding, partnered with desert reclamation coalitions and pivoted its entire R&D strategy. What once seemed like a failure became a foundation. Jonah told his board, "We didn't grow success in fertile ground. It rained where it wasn't supposed to. That's how we know it wasn't us alone."

The wilderness doesn't preclude provision. Sometimes, it prepares us to see where real sustenance comes from.

MY COMPANY'S STORY:
TELL ME WHERE TO SIT?

There was a time in my business when I really needed new clients. I went to a breakfast speaker event at a place I'd never been before. I showed up a little late with another person from our team, and there were only two seats left. I took one of them, not realizing I was sitting right next to the speaker. He turned out to be the Executive Director of a nonprofit, and he was actually looking for a book publisher. That meeting led to us publishing his book, and not just for him personally, but as a brand book project for his whole organization. It was one of our first nonprofit book projects, back in 2019.

Another time, I was invited and attended a business luncheon in place of someone who couldn't make it. There was only one open seat at a large table, so I took it. During introductions, the man next to me mentioned he had three books he wanted to publish. We ended up publishing all three.

These are just two examples—there are many more. God always made sure the right people were put in my path exactly when I needed them.

TRUST THE TABLE IN THE DESERT

What once seemed like a failure became a foundation.

It's easy to believe in God's provision in places that make sense. It's harder to believe He'll set a table in the wilderness, but that's what He does.

"You prepare a table before Me in the presence of My enemies..." (Psalm 23:5)

Not after. Not once the battle is over, but in the middle of the fight. Right there in the dry place. So, if you feel stuck, lost, uncertain, don't panic. You're not forgotten.

Reflection

Are you in a wilderness season right now—emotionally, financially, relationally?

Have you mistaken the wilderness for abandonment?

What would change if you believed God was *already providing* where you are?

Prayer

"Lord, I don't always understand where You've led me, but I trust that You are here. I may not see the provision yet, but I believe it's coming. Open my eyes to how You're providing in unexpected ways. Feed me with peace, provision, and purpose in this dry place. I trust You in the wilderness. Amen."

THE REAL STORY: EXODUS 16:5-30

5 God said to Moses, "I'm going to rain bread down from the skies for you. The people will go out and gather each day's ration. I'm going to test them to see if they'll live according to my Teaching or not. On the sixth day, when they prepare what they have gathered, it will turn out to be twice as much as their daily ration."

6-7 Moses and Aaron told the People of Israel, "This evening you will know that it is God who brought you out of Egypt; and in the morning you will see the Glory of God. Yes, he's listened to your complaints against him. You haven't been complaining against us, you know, but against God."

8 Moses said, "Since it will be God who gives you meat for your meal in the evening and your fill of bread in the morning, it's God who will have listened to your complaints against Him. Who are we in all this? You haven't been complaining to us— you've been complaining to God!"

9 Moses instructed Aaron: "Tell the whole company of Israel: 'Come near to God. He's heard your complaints.'"

10 When Aaron gave out the instructions to the whole company of Israel, they turned to face the wilderness. And there it was: the Glory of God visible in the Cloud.

11-12 God spoke to Moses, "I've listened to the complaints of the Israelites. Now tell them: 'At dusk you will eat meat and at dawn you'll eat your fill of bread; and you'll realize that I am God, *your* God.'"

13-15a That evening quail flew in and covered the camp and in the morning there was a layer of dew all over the camp. When the layer of dew had lifted, there on the wilderness ground was a fine flaky something, fine as frost on the ground. The Israelites took one look and said to one another, *man-hu* (What is it?). They had no idea what it was.

15b-16 So Moses told them, "It's the bread God has given you to eat. And these are God's instructions: 'Gather enough for each person, about two quarts per person; gather enough for everyone in your tent.'"

17-18 The People of Israel went to work and started gathering, some more, some less, but when they measured out what they had gathered, those who gathered more had no extra and those who gathered less weren't short—each person had gathered as much as was needed.

19 Moses said to them, "Don't leave any of it until morning."

20 But they didn't listen to Moses. A few of the men kept back some of it until morning. It got wormy and smelled bad. And Moses lost his temper with them.

21-22 They gathered it every morning, each person according to need. Then the sun heated up and it melted. On the sixth day they gathered twice as much bread, about four quarts per person.

Then the leaders of the company came to Moses and reported.

23-24 Moses said, "This is what God was talking about: Tomorrow is a day of rest, a holy Sabbath to God. Whatever you plan to bake, bake today; and whatever you plan to boil, boil today. Then set aside the leftovers until morning." They set aside what was left until morning, as Moses had commanded. It didn't smell bad and there were no worms in it.

25-26 Moses said, "Now eat it; this is the day, a Sabbath for God. You won't find any of it on the ground today. Gather it every day for six days, but the seventh day is Sabbath; there won't be any of it on the ground."

27 On the seventh day, some of the people went out to gather anyway but they didn't find anything.

28-29 God said to Moses, "How long are you going to disobey my commands and not follow my instructions? Don't you see that God has given you the Sabbath? So on the sixth day, He gives you bread for *two* days. So, each of you, stay home. Don't leave home on the seventh day."

30 So the people quit working on the seventh day.

Chapter Ten

It Never Ran Out

—What You Thought Wasn't Enough

*"The jar of flour was not used up
and the jug of oil did not run dry,
in keeping with the word of the Lord..."*

−1 Kings 17:16

She was down to her last meal. She was a widow, a mother and a famine survivor.

She didn't have a savings account, a 401(k), or even Plan B. What she had was only a handful of flour and a little oil. It was just enough for one more piece of bread, and then in her words, *"We will eat it and die."*

But that's when God sent Elijah to her door. And instead of giving her more food, Elijah asked her to give him all that she had left. He said to her, *"Make me a small cake first, and then something for you and your son."*

Faith is often activated when logic runs dry.

Wait…what?

She's starving. She's stressed. She's at the *end* of everything, not just the end of her rope, and yet she gives. Not because it made sense. Not because she had plenty. But because faith is often activated when logic runs dry. And in that act of obedience, a miracle began.

GOD IS NOT LIMITED BY WHAT YOU LACK

This story reminds us that God doesn't need *a lot* to do *a lot*.

He needs:

- Obedience
- Trust
- Surrender

And that oil? It didn't run out. Day after day, meal after meal, it kept flowing. Enough for the widow, her son, and the prophet during the entire drought. Because when you put what you have into God's hands, He adds to it.

PROFESSIONAL CASE STUDY: FROM EMPTY FRIDGE TO OVERFLOW

Rachelle, a 34-year-old single mom from Boise, had just lost her part-time job during a recession. She had $11 in her bank account and a pantry that wouldn't last the week. Instead of panicking, she tithed her last $10, "not to manipulate God, but because I needed to remind myself who my source was."

The next morning, a former coworker called her out of the blue and asked if she'd be interested in a remote admin contract role. "I just felt like I needed to call you today." It paid double what she'd previously made.

That job turned into a full-time role within 90 days. "It was like the oil never ran out," Rachelle says. "I was afraid to let go of what I had, but when I did, God poured in what I needed."

CORPORATE CASE STUDY:
HYPERSERVE THE MICRO

There was a quiet miracle behind the endurance of EmberSpark Media, a boutique storytelling agency based out of Michigan. In early 2020, as the pandemic dramatically reduced clients across travel, hospitality, and live events, the company's revenue plummeted by 85%. Their biggest retainer canceled. Three employees left.

CEO Renée D. faced facts. By all metrics, they had no runway. But what they *did* have was a team of five deeply committed creatives, laptops and a single contract: a two-week engagement to develop a training video series for a local nonprofit.

Others might have treated the contract as a one-off. Renée treated it like flour in a jar.

She declared a new strategy: *Hyperserve the micro*. Every small client would receive Emmy-level excellence. Scripts would be refined like feature films, visuals handcrafted, edits obsessively polished. If it was the last thing they'd make, it would be legacy-worthy.

But something strange happened. The nonprofit shared the video with its partners. One of them reached out. Then another. Then a regional healthcare foundation commissioned a series, citing EmberSpark's "soulful, resourceful storytelling."

The team never had abundance, but the jar never ran dry. Each week brought just enough. Not much more but always enough.

Renée now calls it *The Provision Model.* It is a principle baked into their culture: quality without extravagance, faithfulness without fatigue and trust that excellence with little can still multiply.

Sometimes, success isn't about what overflows. It's about showing up, when all you have is a scoop and discovering that it's always enough to keep going.

You Might Be Holding a Miracle in Seed Form

Sometimes, the miracle you're praying for is already in your hand.

- A talent you haven't shared

- A relationship you need to reconcile

- A tiny step of obedience

- A gift you've underestimated

- A prayer you keep putting off

The oil won't multiply until it's poured out. God is asking: *"Will you trust Me with the little? Because I'm about to do a lot."*

Reflection

What area of your life feels like it's running out—energy, time, finances?

What's something "small" in your life that God might want to use in a big way?

Are you holding on tightly to something God is asking you to pour out or let go of?

Prayer

"Lord, it feels like I don't have enough, but I trust that You are more than enough. I give You what I have, my resources, my heart and my trust. Multiply it. Stretch it. Use it. Show me that Your oil doesn't run dry when I surrender to You. My lack is no match for Your abundance. Amen."

THE REAL STORY: 1 KINGS 17

1 And then this happened: Elijah the Tishbite, from among the settlers of Gilead, confronted Ahab: "As surely as God lives, the God of Israel before whom I stand in obedient service, the next years are going to see a total drought—not a drop of dew or rain unless I say otherwise."

2-4 God then told Elijah, "Get out of here, and fast. Head east and hide out at the Kerith Ravine on the other side of the Jordan River. You can drink fresh water from the brook; I've ordered the ravens to feed you."

5-6 Elijah obeyed God's orders. He went and camped in the Kerith Canyon on the other side of the Jordan. And sure enough, ravens brought him his meals, both breakfast and supper, and he drank from the brook.

7-9 Eventually the brook dried up because of the drought. Then God spoke to him: "Get up and go to Zarephath in Sidon and live there. I've instructed a woman who lives there, a widow, to feed you."

10-11 So he got up and went to Zarephath. As he came to the entrance of the village he met a woman, a widow, gathering firewood. He asked her, "Please, would you bring me a little water in a jug? I need a drink." As she went to get it, he called out, "And while you're at it, would you bring me something to eat?"

12 She said, "I swear, as surely as your God lives, I don't have so much as a biscuit. I have a handful of flour in a jar and a little oil in a bottle; you found me scratching together just enough firewood to make a last meal for my son and me. After we eat it, we'll die."

13-14 Elijah said to her, "Don't worry about a thing. Go ahead and do what you've said. But first make a small biscuit for me and bring it back here. Then go ahead and make a meal from what's left for you and your son. This is the word of the God of Israel: 'The jar of flour will not run out and the bottle of oil will not become empty before God sends rain on the land and ends this drought.'"

15-16 And she went right off and did it, did just as Elijah asked. And it turned out as he said—daily food for her and her family. The jar of meal didn't run out and the bottle of oil didn't become empty: God's promise fulfilled to the letter, exactly as Elijah had delivered it!

17 Later on the woman's son became sick. The sickness took a turn for the worse—and then he stopped breathing.

18 The woman said to Elijah, "Why did you ever show up here in the first place—a holy man barging in, exposing my sins, and killing my son?"

19-20 Elijah said, "Hand me your son."

He then took him from her bosom, carried him up to the loft where he was staying, and laid him on his bed. Then he prayed, "O God, my God, why have You brought this terrible thing on this widow who has opened her home to me? Why have You killed her son?"

21-23 Three times he stretched himself out full-length on the boy, praying with all his might, "God, my God, put breath back into this boy's body!" God listened to Elijah's prayer and put breath back into his body—he was alive! Elijah picked the boy up, carried him downstairs from the loft, and gave him to his mother. "Here's your son," said Elijah, "alive!"

24 The woman said to Elijah, "I see it all now—you *are* a holy man. When you speak, God speaks—a true word!"

Chapter Eleven

The Dead
Man Walked

—When God Brings the Impossible Back to Life

"Jesus called in a loud voice, 'Lazarus, come out!' The dead man came out..."

–John 11:43–44

By the time Jesus arrived in Bethany, it was too late—at least this is what everyone else thought. Lazarus had already been dead four days, which meant the funeral was over, the tomb was sealed and even the stench of death smelled up the entire village.

Lazarus' sisters, Mary and Martha, loved Jesus and believed in His deity very much. In their urgency, they had sent for Him days earlier. They needed His help desperately but even they had a limit to what they believed could happen.

"Lord, if You had been here, my brother would not have died." (John 11:21)

It's not a lack of love for them to say this but it is the raw grief of a believer caught in a heartbreak. Yes, they believed Jesus could heal. Yes, they didn't yet believe He could resurrect the dead from the living, so what looked dead to them was actually a setup for glory.

GOD IS NEVER LATE. HE'S JUST NOT EARLY.

We don't serve a God who rushes. We don't believe in a God who adheres to our schedule or the schedule of the world. We serve a God who redeems time. This is a concept that is difficult to sometimes believe. For me, there are times as I think of the tremendous hours I've put into the two companies I've been a part of and the hours spent caring for my daughters, I wonder how I may ever get this time back?

Jesus *waited* before going to Lazarus. Of this the scripture is clear. But why did He wait? Why? Because He wasn't interested in a healing that could be debated. He wasn't interested in the "drama" of the death surrounding all. He came to do a resurrection that couldn't be denied. He came to glorify His father and help us see the glory!

"Did I not tell you that if you believe, you will see the glory of God?" (John 11:40)

He called out to the tomb. Not with whispery hope, but with commanding authority. He said, *"Lazarus, come out!"* And with that, death obeyed life. The man who was gone, deemed dead, came walking out—still wrapped in his grave clothes, Lazarus came walking out fully alive.

PROFESSIONAL CASE STUDY: MY MARRIAGE WAS OVER

James and Cynthia, a couple in their mid-40s living in Columbus, OH, were already separated and in the process of divorce. Years of unmet expectations, emotional shutdowns and quiet resentment had built walls between them. They both felt like divorce was the only action.

Cynthia had been praying but felt like it was over. "She said to God, 'If You wanted to fix this, You should've come sooner.'" But one night while journaling, she wrote these unexpected words: *"God can raise dead things."* She texted it to James. And that message became the start of a slow but powerful reconnection. They proceeded to marriage counseling. With tears, apologies, and much prayer. God healed their broken relationship. After a few years they started leading a small group for couples who feel "too far gone," just like the space they were in. James remarked, "Our marriage didn't survive. It resurrected."

CORPORATE CASE STUDY: RESURRECTION SESSIONS

Consider the case of SynergyTech Solutions, a mid-sized software firm that, by 2022, had flatlined in both revenue and morale. The leadership team was divided, innovation had stalled and their latest flagship product had failed miserably in beta testing. Analysts quietly labeled the company a "sunset story," and investors began withdrawing support.

Enter Maria V., a seasoned turnaround strategist who didn't see death—she saw dormancy. "This isn't a failure," she told the remaining leadership in her first meeting. "It's a stasis. And stasis can be reversed." Drawing from what she later referred to as her "Lazarus playbook," Maria began by identifying what was still breathing under the surface: talented engineers, a loyal (though shrinking) client base and a once-pioneering culture.

Her approach wasn't dramatic, it was deliberate. She asked the team not just what went wrong, but what had once made them come alive. She orchestrated what she called "resurrection sessions"—candid workshops where every department revisited its original mission and core values. Slowly, latent creativity stirred. Within eight months, SynergyTech had not only stabilized but launched a revised product that surpassed initial expectations. By the end of the fiscal year, the company posted its first profit in over two years.

Much like the biblical Lazarus, SynergyTech's revival wasn't just about returning from the brink. It was about emerging with renewed clarity and strength. The Lazarus story reminds us that what appears dead may only be waiting for the right voice, the right belief, to call it back.

MY COMPANY'S STORY: HE SENDS YOU BACK

I'll never forget one of the authors we worked with years ago. She was a former stripper, drug addict and even a prostitute who gave her life to Jesus and felt called to go back into the strip clubs to minister to the women still working there. At the time, I remember thinking, *Wow... she's going back into that exact world she came out of to help others?*

It struck me. But over time, I've come to understand it more deeply. God often uses the exact things we've lived through, no matter how painful or messy, to help someone else walk through the same thing. I've seen it in my own life. Parts of my life I once wanted to forget have become the very things that help me connect with others. Because I've been there, really been there, I don't just sympathize, I truly understand. And that's where real empathy and impact begin.

We should, in essence, recognize that our struggles will result in good at times in our lives in the future. This is a fundamental truth I believe!

If It's Not Over, It's Still in Process

Jesus didn't raise *everyone* from the dead, but Lazarus was a signpost of what's possible when God speaks. In your professional life, do you feel like you are standing at the tomb of:

- A calling you gave up on

- A relationship that's got buried somehow

- A business idea you once believed in

- A version of yourself you thought was lost forever

What appears dead may only be waiting for the right voice.

If you've buried something, don't roll the stone in front of your hope just yet. The great news is Jesus is not afraid of tomb. Quite the opposite, He speaks life *into* them. He still calls dead things back to life.

Reflection

What part of your life feels buried or "too far gone"?

Have you stopped praying for something because the timing disappointed you?

What would it look like to stand in front of that tomb with pure, 100% faith, not fear?

Prayer

"Jesus, I've seen things die, dreams, career aspirations, relationships and even peace. But You are the Resurrection and the Life. Speak into every part of me that feels beyond saving. Call me out of hopelessness. Roll away the stone. And teach me to trust that even now, You can do the impossible. Amen."

THE REAL STORY: JOHN 11

1 A man was sick, Lazarus of Bethany, the town of Mary and her sister Martha.

2 This was the same Mary who massaged the Lord's feet with aromatic oils and then wiped them with her hair. It was her brother Lazarus who was sick.

3 So the sisters sent word to Jesus, "Master, the one You love so very much is sick."

4 When Jesus got the message, He said, "This sickness is not fatal. It will become an occasion to show God's glory by glorifying God's Son."

5 Jesus loved Martha and her sister and Lazarus,

6 but oddly, when He heard that Lazarus was sick, He stayed on where He was for two more days.

7 After the two days, He said to his disciples, "Let's go back to Judea."

8 They said, "Rabbi, You can't do that. The Jews are out to kill You, and You're going back?"

9 Jesus replied, "Are there not twelve hours of daylight? Anyone who walks in daylight doesn't stumble because there's plenty of light from the sun.

10 Walking at night, he might very well stumble because he can't see where he's going."

11 He said these things, and then announced, "Our friend Lazarus has fallen asleep. I'm going to wake him up."

12 The disciples said, "Master, if he's gone to sleep, he'll get a good rest and wake up feeling fine."

13 Jesus was talking about death, while his disciples thought he was talking about taking a nap.

14 Then Jesus became explicit: "Lazarus died.

15 And I am glad for your sakes that I wasn't there. You're about to be given new grounds for believing. Now let's go to him."

16 That's when Thomas, the one called the Twin, said to his companions, "Come along. We might as well die with him."

17 When Jesus finally got there, He found Lazarus already four days dead.

18 Bethany was near Jerusalem, only a couple of miles away,

19 and many of the Jews were visiting Martha and Mary, sympathizing with them over their brother.

20 Martha heard Jesus was coming and went out to meet him. Mary remained in the house.

21 Martha said, "Master, if You'd been here, my brother wouldn't have died.

22 Even now, I know that whatever You ask God, He will give You."

23 Jesus said, "Your brother will be raised up."

24 Martha replied, "I know that he will be raised up in the resurrection at the end of time."

25 "You don't have to wait for the End. I am, right now, Resurrection and Life. The one who believes in Me, even though he or she dies, will live.

26 And everyone who lives believing in Me does not ultimately die at all. Do you believe this?"

27 "Yes, Master. All along I have believed that You are the Messiah, the Son of God who comes into the world."

28 After saying this, she went to her sister Mary and whispered in her ear, "The Teacher is here and is asking for you."

29 The moment she heard that, she jumped up and ran out to Him.

30 Jesus had not yet entered the town but was still at the place where Martha had met Him.

31 When her sympathizing Jewish friends saw Mary run off, they followed her, thinking she was on her way to the tomb to weep there.

32 Mary came to where Jesus was waiting and fell at His feet, saying, "Master, if only You had been here, my brother would not have died."

33 When Jesus saw her sobbing and the Jews with her sobbing, a deep anger welled up within Him.

34 He said, "Where did you put him?"

35 Now Jesus wept.

36 The Jews said, "Look how deeply He loved him."

37 Others among them said, "Well, if He loved him so much, why didn't He do something to keep him from dying? After all, He opened the eyes of a blind man."

38 Then Jesus, the anger again welling up within Him, arrived at the tomb. It was a simple cave in the hillside with a slab of stone laid against it.

39 Jesus said, "Remove the stone." The sister of the dead man, Martha, said, "Master, by this time there's a stench. He's been dead four days!"

40 Jesus looked her in the eye. "Didn't I tell you that if you believed, you would see the glory of God?"

41 Then, to the others, "Go ahead, take away the stone.

42 I know You always do listen, but on account of this crowd standing here I've spoken so that they might believe that You sent Me."

43 Then He shouted, "Lazarus, come out!"

44 And he came out, a cadaver, wrapped from head to toe, and with a kerchief over his face. Jesus told them, "Unwrap him and let him loose."

45 That was a turnaround for many of the Jews who were with Mary. They saw what Jesus did, and believed in Him.

Chapter Twelve

In Others –
The Hand of God

CHRISTY VOGEL

SOUNDING JOY FOUNDER / EXECUTIVE DIRECTOR
MARKETING DIRECTION FOUNDER / CEO

I didn't understand God's purpose for my life until my 50s. For years, I carried my pain like armor. Born with hearing loss, I didn't get hearing aids until I was 27. I grew up believing I was stupid, broken, when I was really just unheard. I watched loved ones with the same struggle fall into addiction, and I hardened myself against the world, thinking life had dealt me an unfair hand.

But God.

He opened my eyes to something beautiful: none of it happened *to* me—it happened *for* me. Every setback, every silent classroom, every scar was preparation. He was shaping my heart, giving me the fire to change lives like mine.

In my mid-50s, I followed the calling that I finally heard clearly. I started a nonprofit program to provide hearing aids for children whose families can't afford them.

Now, I wake up every day knowing I'm walking in His purpose. Helping a child hear for the first time? That's holy ground.

God didn't just heal my past—He gave it meaning. And in doing so, He gave me a future far greater than I ever imagined.

Christopher W. Rohe
CEO, GuardianSat

Raised in a Christian Lutheran household, I learned early on that faith is THE compass through life's storms. This foundation guided me in 2020 when I co-founded GuardianSat with Robert Briskman to protect satellites from orbital debris in an increasingly crowded space.

As CEO, my Air Force background and faith-based upbringing anchored me. Facing skepticism during our National Science Foundation grant pursuit, I felt the weight of doubt. In quiet prayer, rooted in the faith instilled by my parents, practiced daily by my children and supported by my wife, I sought God's clarity.

The next morning, a pivotal conversation with a Tampa Bay Wave mentor refined our pitch and direction for our autonomous debris avoidance system, securing a $250,000 grant, and validating our patented technology.

This divine intervention reshaped GuardianSat's path. Our proposed Pathfinder system, enabling real-time satellite protection, gained momentum, earning a Harvard Accelerator win in 2024, ASD Top Ten Space Tech and entry as a finalist in the Global Start-up World Cup in Silicon Valley.

My faith has always shaped my leadership, grounding my decisions in stewardship and integrity in all my business endeavors. GuardianSat's mission to "Keep Space Open" reflects God's call to responsibly care for creation. Faith transforms impossible challenges into opportunities, fueling innovation. I'm honored to share how His greatness guides our mission to safeguard the cosmos for future generations.

Kim Farmer

Founder, Mile High Fitness and Wellness

After working for corporate America as a network engineer for far too long, I realized I couldn't stand one more dull, meaningless, monotonous meeting and decided to take back my life! Well… I got laid off, but I still took my life back! It was probably the best decision I could have made. I mean, really, how many meetings does it take to make a decision?

Not to mention the following things were happening:

- I found myself "sneaking" away from my desk to take walks during the day.

- I would want to exercise at my desk but felt weird about doing it.

- I would try to leave a little early to catch the sunlight to play tennis after work.

- My butt was getting wider. And wider. And wider.

This was obviously a runaway train getting me fat, sick and even more unhappy. I was passionate about fulfilling my purpose, which has always been to help people get healthier.

As a woman of faith, I knew that I was placed here by God to empower people to take their own personal journeys to improved health. I began to investigate what it would take to start teaching fitness classes. I imagined myself on stage, wearing my pink leotard and flipping my hair back in the wind while barking out orders.

It became the most important thing to accomplish, and I was determined that if I could just teach fitness classes (in my leotard), then my bucket list would be complete.

I studied, practiced, took the exam and bam! Just like that I became a Jane Fonda wannabe. Ok, a very dark-skinned Jane, but I did it! As I started to get more knowledgeable on the topic of wellness at work, I dived in and the rest is history. Today, I own Mile High Fitness and Wellness, a national wellness program provider and we are in our seventeenth year. I am passionate about health and wellness and still thoroughly enjoy helping people at work feel better, achieve higher productivity levels and hop a new runaway train to better health.

SAUL GUIMARÃES
CEO, BIMKT

I used to work for one of the biggest health insurance companies in Brazil—Unimed. I was based in Belém, and also traveled often to São Paulo, working as a Marketing Manager.

When I started, the company was in serious financial trouble—over R$260 million in debt. One of my missions was to turn this situation around and achieve positive revenue, and implement some assertive marketing strategies with a low budget. We basically built a company within the company—opening up new positions, training the team, and rebuilding operations from the ground up. It was a huge success.

But behind the scenes, I was working non-stop. My days started around 8 a.m. at the office and sometimes didn't end until 10 p.m. I was also studying hard during this time.

Then, a friend of mine opened two CrossFit boxes, investing around $150,000 USD. But the expected growth didn't come. After a while, he started asking me if I knew a marketing manager to help him.

At first, I didn't. But he kept insisting. Eventually, I said, "What if I help you myself? I'll be your Customer Success Manager." I also brought in two friends—one as an Art Director, the other a Paid Traffic Manager.

And the results were incredible.

In just two months and six days, we increased his revenue by 40%, only using digital marketing. That was when I first saw a real opportunity in this business. This happened in July 2018. And nowadays I know God was just starting plan B.

At the time, I kept working both jobs—still at the health company and also building this new project, which we would later call BI (Business Intelligence Mkt & Com & Tech).

But in September 2018, I was suddenly fired. No explanation, no justification. At that time, I was directly managing a R$11M budget year, and the company was with an annual revenue of R$1.3B, so the work was a huge success. And, it was a month before I got married, with my beautiful and lovely wife. I asked the president why I was being fired, but they never explained. I decided to put everything in God's hands.

I tried applying for other positions, nothing opened up. That's when I truly felt God speaking to me:

"Be courageous. Be a man. Walk this path."

And so I did.

Since then—from 2018 until today—BI has been growing. We're still on the journey. We're not yet where we want to be, but we've come so far. We're working hard, we're passionate, and we're building something with real purpose.

This is not just about business.

This is a calling. This is obedience. This is God's faithfulness.

Andrew J. Cary
CoFounder/CEO
SNAAP™ Transportation

By the time I was 24, I was heading straight to hell. I had racked up arrests, court judgments, and left a trail of destruction. Then in a God-ordained moment, I was pulled from the edge of catastrophe and given a second chance. On July 3, 1986, I surrendered my life to God and have since tried to live in a way that allows Him to guide my choices—whether as a public educator, senior administrator, nonprofit executive, board member, or global strategist and businessman.

Early in my faith journey, someone told me that if I wrote down everything I hoped to accomplish in life, I'd probably be selling myself short. That couldn't have been more true. My own standards were so limited, I would've been content just to stay employed and pay my bills quietly. But God had a much larger purpose for my life.

Since then, I've held leadership roles in education, nonprofits and private industry—including education technology and transportation. Today, I lead one of the most innovative and disruptive personal rapid transit companies set to enter the global market. As CEO, the way I lead and structure the company is grounded in Christian principles. We're not overt or dogmatic about our faith, but we operate by the idea that attraction often speaks louder than promotion.

Over the past five or six years, my faith has grown deeper, and my talents have been stretched far beyond what I imagined. God has provided both the vision and the resources to carry out this work, and I believe the fruits of it are meant to glorify Him. Any financial rewards or success we experience are simply tools to reinvest in the Kingdom.

Ephesians 6:19 has been spoken over my life: "Pray also for me, that whenever I speak, words may be given me so that I will fearlessly make known the mystery of the gospel."

Some may say I'm running from a traditional calling, but I believe marketplace ministry is my assignment. Through the work I do, I strive to express the Gospel—not just with words, but through integrity, vision and impact in every space God places me.

DEBORA A. PORATH
30-YEAR INDEPENDENT SALES DIRECTOR
MARY KAY, INC.

God does something exceptional EVERY day when you call upon Him for direction. Test Him and see. Wake up with no acknowledgement or surrender as to how He wants you to bless. Then wake up another day, acknowledge Him, talk to Him and ask for direction. After acknowledging Him, your day in business will be filled with opportunities to reach higher and He will direct your day. It's important to know you may feel uncomfortable at times but after obedience it will be easy, and the fruits will come.

The feeling after a day of non-surrender will leave a person tired and feeling unaccomplished (basically a waste of a day). The feeling after acknowledging Him when He directs your paths will give you energy and a feeling of not wanting to quit the day but do more and more.

Lift others up, make them feel special, and you will see the fruits of your efforts. Make sure you are giving out with an honest heart and sincere actions, otherwise I believe it will be done in vain.

Just remember, we work for God not man. If you happen to be an entrepreneur is easier to depend on Him for direction so either way "in your ways acknowledge Him, and He shall direct your paths."

Proverbs 3:6

Afterword

My purpose in writing is simply this: that you who believe in God's Son will know beyond the shadow of a doubt that you have eternal life, the reality and not the illusion. That you will know the living God!

This verse from 1 John 5:13 encapsulates the heart of *Tell Them of My Greatness*. It serves as a beacon of hope and assurance, reminding readers that faith in Jesus is not just a fleeting thought but a profound truth that anchors our lives.

As you turn the final pages of this book, may you carry its message with you—a message of greatness, rooted in faith, and destined to inspire your life!

The last bible verse I want to leave you with is this:

1 Peter 4:7-5:14 NLT Translation

The end of the world is coming soon. Therefore, be earnest and disciplined in your prayers. Most important of all, continue to show deep love for each other, for love covers a multitude of sins. ⁹Cheerfully share your home with those who need a meal or a place to stay.

God has given each of you a gift from His great variety of spiritual gifts. Use them well to serve one another. Do you have the gift of speaking? Then speak as though God Himself were speaking through you. Do you have the gift of helping others? Do it with all the strength and energy that God supplies. Then everything you do will bring glory to God through Jesus Christ. All glory and power to Him forever and ever! Amen.

Suffering for Being a Christian

Dear friends, don't be surprised at the fiery trials you are going through, as if something strange were happening to you. ¹³ Instead, be very glad—for these trials make you partners with Christ in His suffering, so that you will have the wonderful joy of seeing His glory when it is revealed to all the world.

If you are insulted because you bear the name of Christ, you will be blessed, for the glorious Spirit of God rests upon you. If you suffer, however, it must not be for murder, stealing, making trouble, or prying into other people's affairs. But it is no shame to suffer for being a Christian. Praise God for the privilege of being called by His name! For the time has come for judgment, and it must begin with God's household. And if judgment begins with us, what terrible fate awaits those who have never obeyed God's Good News? And also,

"If the righteous are barely saved,
what will happen to godless sinners?"

So if you are suffering in a manner that pleases God, keep on doing what is right, and trust your lives to the God who created you, for He will never fail you.

So humble yourselves under the mighty power of God, and at the right time He will lift you up in honor. Give all your worries and cares to God, for He cares about you.

Stay alert! Watch out for your great enemy, the devil. He prowls around like a roaring lion, looking for someone to devour. Stand firm against him, and be strong in your faith. Remember that your family of believers all over the world is going through the same kind of suffering you are.

In his kindness God called you to share in His eternal glory by means of Christ Jesus. So after you have suffered a little while, He will restore, support, and strengthen you, and He will place you on a firm foundation. All power to him forever! Amen.

Peace be with all of you who are in Christ.

About the Author

Liza Marie Garcia is a powerhouse of purpose and publishing— a former tech CEO turned award-winning author, media strategist and founder of NOW Global Media Group. Based in Tampa, Florida, she leads CEO Book Publishing, a division that has produced over 80 titles and empowered hundreds of emerging voices across business, leadership, entrepreneurship and technology, and faith-based storytelling. With vision and resilience, her team expanded  during the COVID-19 pandemic, releasing works across more than 20 genres including brand books, memoirs, journals, poetry and children's literature.

As a six-time author and serial entrepreneur, Liza Marie's literary journey began with *Never Drink Coffee During a Business Meeting*, featured on Barnes & Noble's 2016 West Coast book tour. She's co-authored titles including *My Calendar is Written in Crayon*, *The 90-*

Day Author, Top 25 Changemakers, Wisdom Before Me and *Leaving Stronger Than You Started.*

This September, she unveils her seventh and most powerful work to date: *Tell Them of My Greatness.* Poised to inspire thousands, the book will be spotlighted in Barnes & Noble stores and tours nationwide—continuing her tradition of delivering bold, faith-infused narratives that speak to both heart and hustle.

Liza Marie launched her career at IBM as a software design engineer, and by 27 she became one of the youngest founders of a professional services firm in the U.S. telecommunications industry. She scaled her company across Seattle and Portland before settling in Tampa Bay. Today, she mentors startups through the Tampa Bay Wave and contributes to the community through philanthropy and leadership.

Her media footprint includes hosting her own Roku channel, producing podcasts and leading the Tampa region of Faith Driven Entrepreneurs, alongside past leadership roles with Christian Professionals Tampa, Gatekeepers International and Christian Business Fellowship.

Beyond the boardroom, Liza Marie is the proud mother of two brilliant college daughters, an avid pickleball player, marathon finisher and self-declared USTA tennis enthusiast. Her unwavering strength is rooted in her deep faith. "Jesus is the head of my household," she declares. "I will serve the Lord."

Connect with the Author

in   linkedin.com/in/lizamariegarcia/

YouTube   youtube.com/@lizamariegarciaCEO

⊙   instagram.com/lizagarciaceo/

⊙   instagram.com/ceobookpub/

f   facebook.com/ceobookpublishing

⊕   CeoBookPublishing.com

⊕   LizaMarieGarcia.com

DO YOU WANT TO HEAR FROM HIM?

DO YOU WANT TO GET TO KNOW HIM?

There are many names for God in the bible. You should research them. Here are a few I love:

El-Shaddai

Adonai

Jehovah Jireh

Make No Mistake, He is just waiting for you to ask!

Ask Him Today!